I Feel Sorry
for God

O. GENE BICKNELL

WESTBOW
PRESS®
A DIVISION OF THOMAS NELSON
& ZONDERVAN

This book is a work of non-fiction. Unless otherwise noted, the author and the publisher make no explicit guarantees as to the accuracy of the information contained in this book and in some cases, names of people and places have been altered to protect their privacy.

WestBow Press books may be ordered through booksellers or by contacting:

WestBow Press
A Division of Thomas Nelson & Zondervan
1663 Liberty Drive
Bloomington, IN 47403
www.westbowpress.com
844-714-3454

Scripture quotations marked KJV are taken from the King James Version.

Scripture quotations marked NASB are taken from The New American Standard Bible®, Copyright © 1960, 1962, 1963, 1968, 1971, 1972, 1973, 1975, 1977, 1995 by The Lockman Foundation. Used by permission.

ISBN: 978-1-6642-3025-5 (sc)
ISBN: 978-1-6642-3026-2 (hc)
ISBN: 978-1-6642-3027-9 (e)

Library of Congress Control Number: 2021907201

Print information available on the last page.

WestBow Press rev. date: 07/26/2021

THE BIBLE SCRIPTURES REFERENCED IN THIS BOOK ARE FROM THE King James version, and my opinions and what I took away personally from reading the scriptures. I also read the American Standard version and other bible translations. I am only making the information to relate to "feeling sorry for God." Any use of copywritten sections is not my knowledge! This is my attempt to explain why we should "feel sorry for God."

Prelude

I FEEL SORRY FOR GOD BECAUSE WE CAUSE HIM PAIN, BUT I FEEL more sorry for those who miss the wonderful time in His Kingdom. I know what the Kingdom is like! I've had the vision. Living with the Holy Spirit is so, so, so comforting.

Please don't let me feel sorry for you.

Vision

When God gives you the vision of Heaven, you will not want yourself to be felt sorry for! The interesting thing about prayer is that it can be comforting. Celebrities should listen. Those who promote their own worth or set themselves up as feeling like they're special are in danger of putting themselves in a position to let their ego make them in losing their relationship with God and they may be brought to their knees, not to demonstrate but by falling out of the grace of God. They will feel sorry for themselves!

God expects us to be humble. Treat others as equals and ask for God to help them be disciples of our Lord. When you rebel or try to impose your will on others, you are forgetting that God intended for us to be charitable and not self-centered.

Supporting controversy is requiring that you know all the facts and not by emotions. The world is filled with Satan followers. It's easy to do what "feels good" and not supported by God.

When our country was founded under God, God smiled and He watched over us and protected us. That may be coming to an end! God is disturbed and saddened by us in this country, the most wonderful country in the world. Wouldn't you hate to have to leave these United Stated founded by God?

Preface

THIS BOOK IS NOT WRITTEN FOR THE DEVOUT, THE TRUE Believers, the Loyal Subject of God's Word, although they may find these words influenced by God Himself.

This book is about God and understanding we don't make it easy for Him!

How He so wants us to be worthy of the Promises of Christ.

The intent is to inform that God deserves some concern from us. Not only does He alone rule and control, but it's difficult to deal with a world (billions of people) who ask and receive so much from Him, but never consider how tough it might be for Him.

I don't want to sound unstable, but I'm doing this writing with God's assistance. All profits go to God's work. He is still consistent in wanting to fill His Heavens with true believers and followers. That's why He gives us chance after chance to become worthy.

God opened the doors to Heaven, but the doors must be available through His Son, Jesus Christ.

You must believe that Jesus is the Son of God. Some of you still need to accept that!

Enjoy God's Words!
O. Gene Bicknell

I'm writing this book with God's help! Not for believers or followers of Christ, but for those folks who haven't found peace in life because God's love is missing in their lives. The comfort that comes from believing and becoming God's person. The worries of your life that can be turned over to God and leaving your troubles and problems for God to take care of.

I won't have to feel sorry for God or for you when you find Him. You become one of God's children and maybe help someone else that we have to feel sorry for. That's how God can fill His Heavens, one at a time or groups of followers.

It's easy to be followers, and life's aches and pains are in the Lord's hands.

Take the time to hear why, "I feel sorry for God." He tries so hard and forgives so easy. No grudges for you or from Him. How can His love be so strong?

Part of my ministry is to make us understand who God is ...

We pray and praise the higher Power, but do we understand Him?

He tells us and sends messages of Himself, and in Exodus 20:5, you shall not bow down to idols or serve them! For I, the Lord your God am a jealous God! Inequities are also mentioned. There is no equal for all people, kings, wealth, slave, leader, follower, or beggar. We are all different in status and God plans if that way.

What is He saying to us?

Some hate God or ignore Him. Some believe they can do as they please and ask forgiveness and all is well.

Psalm 37:13 (KJV) says the Lord laughs at the wicked, He knows their day is coming.

Do you not know that God knows us personally? He knows you well. Everything about you!! When you were born, why, purpose, etc.

Hard to understand how God can keep each of us in His sight. Think!

Insignificant? No! You're not!

You're His child, deeply love. He cares! You hurt Him! We all do, but more than us, His threshold is higher. Forgiving ... unreasonably so! His arms are always open. The pain He's suffered. Jesus' sacrifice but before Adam, Eve, Cain, disruption of His plans ... His Glory-Kingdom-Power. The greatest gift to us – Love. NB!!!

God converses with me at times, at least I feel His presence. He gave me the project, "The Shrine of the Holy Spirit," in Branson, Missouri. God gave me the writing of the book, "The Personal Side of God." And He gave this book, "I feel Sorry for God," providing the material. I felt compelled to do all. Zealot, no I don't think so. But how could anyone ignore God? The evidence of His creation is there. The comfort of following Him is "splendid."

I leave these thoughts and experiences to my descendants and those who know me.

Sins caused me stress and worry. Faith gives me comfort and pride. As a deacon, trustee, moderator, servant, and prayer warrior, life is much simpler and my regrets for failure as a father, friend, and spouse is somewhat forgiven by God ... but it's hard to forgive yourself. Those who I've offended throughout my life can't be changed, but I'll keep praying for forgiveness!

If my family and those I care about will follow the path with God, I'll be more blessed than I am today. And ... I'm amazingly blessed today!!

In Christ, Dad, Husband, Friend, and Relative - O. Gene Bicknell

hapter 1

I FEEL SORRY FOR GOD THAT HE MUST USE HIS FURY TO GET OUR attention. Natural disasters to us are His weapons to show "He is in Control." He sees all, knows all, hears all! We can't do anything or believe anything that He doesn't know! Humans brag about strengths, power, ability to develop strength. Powerful bombs, guns, military forces, defense systems, strong structure, etc. We'll rebuild the World Trade Center, we'll be impregnable, they won't be able to overcome our defenses and strengths. We, We, We!!!

Never once mentioning the need for God's help to defend us! Nothing is a s strong or as powerful as God's ...

If nations that think your military strength is great, think again ... one little virus can shut down and destroy the world's economy. "One."

God has all weather, storms, tsunamis, lightening, darkness, fire, plagues. See Joel (another example of the past) earthquakes and using weaker countries with His might to defeat stronger and more powerful ones. David, a boy, not big and strong as Goliath, destroys the huge warrior.

God is a by-word to many. God warns us time after time.

His favorite people, the Israelites, spent 40 years in bondage after being warned time after time. The Assyrians battled them once and were driven away. The first terrorists, the Assyrians, after the Israelites went back to ignoring God and next battle defeated the Israelites. The Israelites seem to never learn. In the book of Amos, Chapter 1 and 3 (KJV) 3-8 all God's wrath. In chapter 9 – God restores hope. Even today the Jewish Israelites don't realize that as chosen people, the Lord wants them to protect each other. They elect politicians that aren't supportive of their chosen country. Jerusalem is the place God wants His temple.

God will continue to warn! God will continue to offer forgiveness, and protection, but only if we recognize and obey His Word!

Ebola, plague, storms, weapons of God should show you that the Almighty is with us daily. There's no escape from His knowledge of us, each one of us are in the sight and expectations of our Heavenly Father. A kind Father, a loving Father, but a powerful Father, who will only put up with so much; then watch out!! He will punish those of us who sin and won't repent ... who let themselves be more important than their Maker?

We are like a board game to God. He sees all the pieces and players in the game and watches how they play the game of life. We better decide Heaven or hell, learn or avoid, peacemakers or obstructers. "Your right to choose" is a valid opportunity to avoid the inevitable. You will decide: punishment for disobedience or reward for following.

Disciples, as we become when reality sets in and we realize God knows all, sees all, forgiveness available and the reward is wonderful. Praise to be the Lord who is Almighty and forgiving. For He is parallel in His desire to fill His Heavens.

If you loved the Lord like God loves you, you wouldn't want to hurt Him, cause Him grief, or cause Him to be upset with you by your disobedient and wayward ways.

God is present in your life. He is here and He will always be here. Watching and observing you, whether you like it or not. You can react to this in any way you want ... it's totally your choice. The Lord is accustomed to rejection and being ignored. It's nothing new to Him. He would rather you acknowledge Him and recognize His presence, but He knows and understands that some will praise Him, and some won't even care whether He's there or not! I feel sorry for them and I feel sorry for God, because He continues to care about us.

Oh, how we wish we had more friends like the Lord. What a wonderful world it could be! That "could be" world does exist! It's called the Kingdom of God! God is here every day to let us know that that Kingdom has a door through the sacrifice of His Son.

God and His Holy Spirit are always here at arm's length. Yes, that close!

Surely you don't think that God made Heavens and earth and walked away? His great creation being left alone and walked away? Think about that ... He is interested and committed. He continues to watch us always. He has the power to make us miserable or happy. He can provide whatever we need or ask for if He wants. God's power through supernatural strength can destroy us or give us pleasures or discomforts. Those powers hang over our heads! We can find His grace, or we can find His wrath. He's given us the right to choose! Use it wisely, but make no mistake, He is in charge!

You can have your earthly fun, and Satan will lead you to sin. Undermining God's will has been his focus since God created us.

We all sin, some small sins, and others bigger sins. No matter what or how big or small, God offers repentance and restitution! Oh, how Great to have a loving God.

Love is the lifeline to happiness. Finding love is our challenge! I suggest you start with the remarkable chance that God opens His arms for a warm "hug" whenever we ask for one. God loves a loving hug!! How comforting to have the Hands of God and His Holy Spirit and Son waiting for their "hug" too! I need 40 hugs a day and I'm always grateful to all my earthly contacts to give me a "hug" as well to fill my heart with 40 "hugs." Try it, you'll like it!

I had an annual golf celebrity charity tournament for 15 years. Forty or more celebrities every year. A hundred sponsors, big corporations, and other business organizations. Lots of spectators and players donating time and money. It was successful and showcased our city. Volunteers worked year-round to prepare for it. My job was to be host!

Every celebrity, worker, and player all got hugs from me when they arrived. Some of the male celebrities were not used to getting a hug. On the Saturday night banquet of the three-day event, I gave each of the celebrities the microphone to speak for a few minutes. "Foots" Walker, a former professional basketball player, whose two kids and wife were fantastic and beautiful people were there when Foots took the mic and said, "It's nice to be here, the people all support this fundraiser." He said, "I showed up and was greeted by some white dude that gave me a 'hug.'" (Laughter) He said, "You know, I liked it! Thanks, Gene, for having me."

God was with us. He blessed us every year. New friendships were forged. Some of the biggest celebrities in the world blended with the locals, and everyone showed respect and love for God's work.

This book is focused on thinking about "God Himself."

hapter 2

LET'S THINK ABOUT THE EXTENT OF HOW FAR GOD WILL GO AND the patience He shows in the process of getting His plans accomplished. When He sent Moses to Egypt to free His chosen people from 40 years of slavery, God had to use supernatural methods to convince the Pharaoh to agree to release them. The snake from the staff, turning river into blood, sickness, sores, and finally convincing him to release them.

What about Moses' thoughts and the failure of many negotiations that failed with the Pharaoh? God had to cause extreme circumstances before the Israelites were freed. Moses could have been killed as well. Of course God was protecting Aaron and Moses. God could have destroyed Egypt, but He chose as His way, the negotiation process.

Also, think about Nehemiah when as a servant of the king had to ask for permission to leave for Judah to rebuild the temple (he could have been put to death if the king didn't grant him leave and assistance). He knew the risk. The King, Artaxerxes granted him assistance, protection of soldiers, and passes to get through the other countries and maintain timber for building. God was with Nehemiah, the humble servant of the king.

When we read scripture, it's enlightening and informative and pleasurable to learn. Not just words, but the emotions behind the words and what the individuals involved were thinking and their loyalty by faith. Understand more than the message or story.

God warns us in many ways, and He gives us the opportunity to fully understand.

Now, as we face a coronavirus that changes the course of daily living around the world. Is this a warning against defying God's presence; and for ignoring God's presence? Just know that God has all the most devastating weapons at His disposal. Disease, storms, winds lightening, earthquakes, temperature, fires, and the outer space projectiles that could hammer the earth. Nothing mankind can create can equal God's Power. The only total protection from anything is to be protected by the Almighty Father.

It's comforting to know that He can save us from anything He wants us protected from.

Nehemiah and all of God's servants know that without God's help, their mission will not or would not be successful. With the assistance from the king and together with the Israelites, the walls of the temple and the gates were rebuilt and finished.

If the people and the governments would only try the help of God, can we accomplish the difficult challenges we face.

The coronavirus has startling effect on the entire world. Economic collapse! All sections of the world are in a defensive and research mode to combat it. "I believe this is God's way to show who's really in charge!!" We need a worldly day of prayer and ask for God's help. We're busy trying to protect ourselves and seeking a cure and not realizing we may need God's help ...

Mankind is smart and does great things in every field and organization, but nothing is as powerful as God's Will!

One hundred and six billion (106,000,000,000) have walked on the earth in the last 50,000 years.

Today 7,564,000,000 now walk on the earth. This increases rapidly every day. God's Kingdom will hold all that pass through and find favor from the Lord. What happens to the others? You don't want to know …

God doesn't change! He's parallel in His intent; He's consistent! He says in the KJV of Malachi, "Return to Me, and I'll return to you!"

God's wrath can be terrifying. His power is above all the weapons of war and destruction. In Deuteronomy 9:22 (KJV), it is exposed. Storms, supernatural powers, stronger than any nation can defend.

Be sure we know that God is in control! Any powerful nation may think their military is invincible but will vanish if God so desires.

God still loves us in ways we cannot fathom, Jeremiah 31:3 (KJV).

The first step of rebuilding a nation is the building of a great wall. God instructed Nehemiah to build a wall around Jerusalem to protect its citizens from enemy attacks. The U.S. is building a wall to protect its citizens from illegal attacks.

God relies on leaders to do His work. They cannot stop what God wants you to hear and understand.

There is more behind the bible verses than just words! Go through your mind and put yourself in the picture. What was Abraham going through when the son he loved, and he had wanted for so long, and he was asked to sacrifice. Isaac, who he loved so dearly, to go beyond human emotion and slay your own son for a sacrifice to prove your love of God (God too, when He sent Jesus). Isaac was old enough to realize what his dad was going to do. (Think about this; not just the words).

How Noah felt when he couldn't take his friends and relatives knowing they would die.

About Job when his lovely family and holdings were being taken away. Think beyond the words. How Jonah couldn't hide from God (what were his thoughts?). How do I keep from doing God's request?

We must realize that God is here. Our Father is a whisper away and He doesn't hear from us. He is not a far-away redeemer, or a distant feature. He is right there waiting to hear your request and ready to listen. Even though He knows we don't always listen to Him! He has many ways to perform towards us, but He may not act quickly, or even on our requests. They are still in His mind and He's totally aware of the pros and cons of helping us in our problems.

We need to ask and pray for what we need. We say that we are not saying that some of us are worth more than others, but simply that the Creator has control over the created. It's all about being dependent on "Him." Temptation is present, pride is there, and personal achievement is important, and not just in material form, but in the heart with motivation toward pleasing God.

In Hosea, we learn of God's intentions to restore His people, including gentiles, into His family.

On one side, there is the law of God through Moses. On the other side, there is the Good News from Jesus and not just the law is needed; but the belief and following the promises of Jesus, because the door to Heaven is Jesus.

# Chapter 3

Why?

The deepest level of worship is praising God through the pain, thanking God during the trials, trusting Him when we're tempted to lose hope, and loving Him, even when He seems distant.

At my lowest, God is my hope.
At my darkest, God is my light.
At my weakest, God is my strength.
At my saddest, God is my comforter.

GOD HAS SHOWN HIS STRENGTH AND POWERS TO HIS PEOPLE through centuries, and even miracles do not reach the greatest recognition in the hearts of all mankind. This is God willing to create love and acceptance for redemption. WHY IS THAT NOT OBVIOUS?

How disappointed is our Father? I feel sorry He can't reach all souls. God shows His disappointment through Elijah when He tells Elijah to speak God's words. God tells Elijah this is what he should do! Elijah asks on Mount Carmel to bring the 450 prophets of Baal, the God they worship, to bring the two sacrifices. This challenge is Elijah's way to prove the true God.

God now, today is needing to prove once again that He is still our living God. We don't worship Baal, but immorality, sinful nature is breaking God's laws for us. We need to be reminded that God is in charge. I believe God will give us signs and acts of His power in the coming months. I'm sorry God is placed in this position again! Hopefully, we'll listen to God's Words.

1 Kings 18:20-46 (NASB 1995) "20 So Ahab sent a message among all the sons of Israel and brought the prophets together at Mount Carmel. 21 Elijah came near to all the people and said, "How long will you hesitate between two opinions? If the Lord is God, follow Him; but if Baal, follow him." But the people did not answer him a word. 22 Then Elijah said to the people, "I alone am left a prophet of the Lord, but Baal's prophets are 450 men. 23 Now let them give us two oxen; and let them choose one ox for themselves and cut it up, and place it on the wood, but put no fire under it; and I will prepare the other ox and lay it on the wood, and I will not put a fire under it. 24 Then you call on the name of your god, and I will call on the name of the Lord, and the God who answers by fire, He is God." And all the people said, "That is a good idea."

25 So Elijah said to the prophets of Baal, "Choose one ox for yourselves and prepare it first for you are many, and call on the name of your god, but put no fire under it." 26 Then they took the ox which was given them and they prepared it and called on the name of Baal from morning until noon saying, "O Baal, answer us." But there was no voice and no one answered. And they leaped about the altar which they made. 27 It came about at noon, that Elijah mocked them and said, "Call out with a loud voice, for he

is a god; either he is occupied or gone aside, or is on a journey, or perhaps he is asleep and needs to be awakened." 28 So they cried with a loud voice and cut themselves according to their custom with swords and lances until the blood gushed out on them. 29 When midday was past, they raved until the time of the offering of the evening sacrifice; but there was no voice, no one answered, and no one paid attention.

30 Then Elijah said to all the people, "Come near to me." So all the people came near to him. And he repaired the altar of the Lord which had been torn down. 31 Elijah took twelve stones according to the number of the tribes of the sons of Jacob, to whom the word of the Lord had come, saying, "Israel shall be your name." 32 So with the stones he built an altar in the name of the Lord, and he made a trench around the altar, large enough to hold two measures of seed. 33 Then he arranged the wood and cut the ox in pieces and laid it on the wood. 34 And he said, "Fill four pitchers with water and pour it on the burnt offering and on the wood." And he said, "Do it a second time," and they did it a second time. And he said, "Do it a third time," and they did it a third time. 35 The water flowed around the altar and he also filled the trench with water.

36 At the time of the offering of the evening sacrifice, Elijah the prophet came near and said, "O Lord, the God of Abraham, Isaac and Israel, today let it be known that You are God in Israel and that I am Your servant and I have done all these things at Your word. 37 Answer me, O Lord, answer me, that this people may know that You, O Lord, are God, and that You have turned their heart back again." 38 Then the fire of the Lord fell and consumed the burnt offering and the wood and the stones and the dust, and licked up the water that was in the trench. 39 When all the people

saw it, they fell on their faces; and they said, "The Lord, He is God; the Lord, He is God." 40 Then Elijah said to them, "Seize the prophets of Baal; do not let one of them escape." So they seized them; and Elijah brought them down to the brook Kishon, and slew them there.

41 Now Elijah said to Ahab, "Go up, eat and drink; for there is the sound of the roar of a heavy shower." 42 So Ahab went up to eat and drink. But Elijah went up to the top of Carmel; and he crouched down on the earth and put his face between his knees. 43 He said to his servant, "Go up now, look toward the sea." So he went up and looked and said, "There is nothing." And he said, "Go back" seven times. 44 It came about at the seventh time, that he said, "Behold, a cloud as small as a man's hand is coming up from the sea." And he said, "Go up, say to Ahab, 'Prepare your chariot and go down, so that the heavy shower does not stop you.'" 45 In a little while the sky grew black with clouds and wind, and there was a heavy shower. And Ahab rode and went to Jezreel. 46 Then the hand of the Lord was on Elijah, and he girded up his loins and outran Ahab to Jezreel." We must listen to what the Lord Says. Listen and believe that your future depends on it!!!

There are many opportunities to wonder about the biblical people. Mary, mother of God. What about her parents, who were they? They're not mentioned in the scriptures.

What about Joseph, Jesus' earthly father? What about Joseph's family? They're not mentioned or any information about them. What was Joseph doing throughout Jesus' life? Did Jesus learn Joseph's trade while growing up? Were there ever any disciples needed (probably not) for God's Son? What happened to Jesus? Did He have friends? What about Jesus' siblings? We hear of James, His brother, but not much.

You can't be recognized as an expert or a special person sometimes when people grow up with you and have a life the same as yours. If you know someone well and you interact with them daily, it's not always easy to see their characteristics. Therefore Jesus' growing up was probably just an ordinary person to His friends and playmates. When His ministry started, He was in Canaan and performed His first miracle. When Mother Mary said to Him, the wine is running out; Jesus said, my time has not yet come. These are my take of the scriptures.

These factors are not influencing any changes as to what occurred, but curiosity is in many persons minds and they're interested. This is true about your neighbors and friends. Your parents, events of your siblings' lives that you don't know about. Your parents you don't know about. One of my brothers saw combat in World War II. A medic who went into the invasion of Saipan and Okinawa, he had buddies shot and killed right next to him. He had bad memories and battle fatigue.   They call it PTSD now. He was never treated. I spent a year by his side to make sure he didn't kill someone. He had anger and nervous stress that caused him to explode over sometimes minor occurrences. He would never talk about his war experiences. He was nine years older, and I worried about him. There were five of us boys, and he was the second oldest boy. He is the reason I went to college young. He had the G.I. Bill and went to college and worked the rest of his time. He was awarded a degree to teach, but never did. He was a butcher, and later opened two grocery stores that he owned. An entrepreneur who never overcame the effects of the war. I always wondered what he went through. When in the Pacific Islands, he sent pictures of scenes after the battle, with dead bodies still on the ground.

My mom was 75% Native American. My great grandmother was on the Trail of Tears with her two-year-old daughter (my grandmother) from the Carolinas to Oklahoma. Nearly half of them died on the march. My mother was born on the reservation in Oklahoma. My grandfather was a doctor. Not from a medical school, but you could take a test to prove your medical knowledge and get licensed to practice. Doc Moses Grazier … he was a scoundrel. He had practiced on the reservation and married Martha Ellena Ballard Grazier, who was pregnant with my mom. Doc Moses also had a practice in Kansas and was married to a white woman. He was challenged by the Cherokee in court about his behavior but managed to get away with it. The white woman's baby died at birth, and my mom was born on the reservation about the same time. My grandfather didn't want my mom to live and grow up as an Indian. Indians were considered to be a race unworthy of respect, and prejudice toward them caused them to be persecuted and biased more than blacks. Black Lives Matter yells racist to white people to divide our nation. Satan leads them. My people learned to live with prejudice. Some companies wouldn't hire white men if they were married to an Indian. I witnessed this persecution and Grandfather Moses was aware that mom's life would be better if she were considered Caucasian.

I didn't know this growing up and mom never ever mentioned it in our presence. I didn't learn until I was an adult. I don't even know how mom and dad met, except that a relative was related to both of them, so through family ties they would have met. But I wasn't even interested until I was writing about our family of most of the people who knew them were dead. Mom didn't have any proof of her birth and it is not on the Cherokee Tribal Rolls, even though her grandmother and mother are on the rolls and also her brothers, sisters, and cousins. Mom wasn't registered on the Cherokee rolls even though she was named after her mother, Martha Ellena Ballard Grazier. Mom was Martha Ellen Grazier Bicknell.

We don't have a lot of information about my ancestors. I never thought about my ancestors because being born younger than most of my siblings and never meeting any of my grandparents, I wasn't inspired to ask about lineage. When I started to write, I was sorry I didn't know much except what I heard in some family discussions.

So ... I'm sorry that I don't know a lot about who my ancestors or their descendants were. Never do I judge a person by what I see or hear. They may have demons fighting them. Or the truth may be distorted. The stories are handed down through the generations and accuracy could be questioned.

 hapter 4

GOD IS DIFFERENT. HE KNOWS US COMPLETELY AND THERE ARE no questions of accuracy. God can clarify, we can't always do that. So we must love by faith. God smiles when He sees our acceptance and love for Him, our families, and friends.

He is disappointed when we put restrictions or conditions on our love. I feel sorry for those who have the chance to love unconditionally.

Temptation is a constant pressure on our daily lives. Lucifer and his followers created their own evil place. They have been undermining God's Will ever since they were cast out of God's Kingdom. The evil is present every day and everywhere. They are trying to get all of us to do sin and disobey God. Their influence gives us desire to take the pleasures of sin. God no longer can change our free will, distractions by sin, but the influence of Satan's evil urging of us to justify doing the sin. It's up to us to accept God's love and find the promises of Christ.

Being with friends, guys with the guys and girls (women) being with the girls, having fun doing fun things together. The mix may be boys and girls. Young or old. These gatherings or activities may offer temptation to sin. God knows that He understands the world and all the circumstances. He also knows we're humans and have human weaknesses. You don't have to be a "stick in the mud." God wants you to have fun and joy in your life! He just wants your heart and logic to realize that if you sin, it's not the end of the world. Thanks for God's love but know that the price of sin is far greater than the fun you think you had sinning. You can recover from rejection, but the sentence and regrets are sometimes devastating. Plus, you can have fun and joyful experiences without sinning to do it. Over 30 million of God's creation have been aborted because of undesired pregnancies.

There are demons and evil spirit around us all over the world. They are ready to take us into evil and sinful things. Tempt us and put thoughts in our heads that one little sin can give you pleasure, so why would it hurt to have a little fun? You are encouraged to think that it's okay to do what you know is wrong and you deserve a little fun or get something you really want. After all, you've been good, and one time won't hurt anything. It's so easy to procrastinate and find excuse for doing what's open for you … All sins are paid for some time and some way. Stress, guilt, exposed, caught, always punished.

In the KJV of 1 Samuel 2, Hannah prayed:

> The Lord has filled my heart with joy (give thanks)
> I feel very strongly in the Lord
> I can laugh at my enemies
> I am glad because you have helped me

There is no one Holy like the Lord

Recognize there is no God but your God (not wealth-power-material-possessions)

There is no rock like our God

Don't continue bragging
Don't speak proud words (be humble as God praises)
The Lord is a God that knows everything
And He judges what people do
The bows of warriors' break
But weak people become strong
Those who once had plenty of food now must ask for God's help
But people who were hungry are hungry no more

The woman who couldn't have children ever is sad (God's power to cry)

But the woman who had many children now is sad depending only on her behavior.
The Lord sends death and He brings life (God)
He sends people to the grave and He raises them to life again (God's plan; poor and rich; king and slave)

Some people humble, others He makes great

The Lord raised the poor up from the dust
He lifts the needy from the ashes

He lets the poor sit with princes and receives a
throne of honor

The foundation of the earth belongs to the Lord and

    The Lord set the world upon them (Adam and Eve)
    He protects those who are loyal to Him
    But evil people will be silenced in darkness
    Power is not the key to success! (heart)
    The Lord destroys His enemies; He will thunder
    in Heaven against them
    The Lord will judge all the earth
    He will give power to His king
    And make His appointed king strong.

In Proverbs 10 and 11 (KJV), message of good and evil (idol worship; rejected).

"Identity" Scripture Passages

2 Corinthians 5:17 (KJV)
Therefore if any man be in Christ, he is a new creature: old things are passed away; behold, all things are become new.

Galatians 2:20 (KJV)
I am crucified with Christ: nevertheless I live; yet not I, but Christ liveth in me: and the life which I now live in the flesh I live by the faith of the Son of God, who loved me, and gave himself for me.

Deuteronomy 7:6 (KJV)

For thou art an holy people unto the Lord thy God: the Lord thy God hath chosen thee to be a special people unto himself, above all people that are upon the face of the earth.

Psalm 106:33-109:31 (KJV)

106:33 Because they provoked his spirit, so that he spake unadvisedly with his lips.

34 They did not destroy the nations, concerning whom the Lord commanded them:

35 But were mingled among the heathen, and learned their works.

36 And they served their idols: which were a snare unto them.

37 Yea, they sacrificed their sons and their daughters unto devils,

38 And shed innocent blood, even the blood of their sons and of their daughters, whom they sacrificed unto the idols of Canaan: and the land was polluted with blood.

39 Thus were they defiled with their own works, and went a whoring with their own inventions.

40 Therefore was the wrath of the Lord kindled against his people, insomuch that he abhorred his own inheritance.

41 And he gave them into the hand of the heathen; and they that hated them ruled over them.

42 Their enemies also oppressed them, and they were brought into subjection under their hand.

43 Many times did he deliver them; but they provoked him with their counsel, and were brought low for their iniquity.

44 Nevertheless he regarded their affliction, when he heard their cry:

45 And he remembered for them his covenant, and repented according to the multitude of his mercies.

46 He made them also to be pitied of all those that carried them captives.

47 Save us, O Lord our God, and gather us from among the heathen, to give thanks unto thy holy name, and to triumph in thy praise.

48 Blessed be the Lord God of Israel from everlasting to everlasting: and let all the people say, Amen. Praise ye the Lord.

107:1 O give thanks unto the Lord, for he is good: for his mercy endureth for ever.

2 Let the redeemed of the Lord say so, whom he hath redeemed from the hand of the enemy;

3 And gathered them out of the lands, from the east, and from the west, from the north, and from the south.

4 They wandered in the wilderness in a solitary way; they found no city to dwell in.

5 Hungry and thirsty, their soul fainted in them.

6 Then they cried unto the Lord in their trouble, and he delivered them out of their distresses.

7 And he led them forth by the right way, that they might go to a city of habitation.

8 Oh that men would praise the Lord for his goodness, and for his wonderful works to the children of men!

9 For he satisfieth the longing soul, and filleth the hungry soul with goodness.

10 Such as sit in darkness and in the shadow of death, being bound in affliction and iron;

11 Because they rebelled against the words of God, and contemned the counsel of the most High:

12 Therefore he brought down their heart with labour; they fell down, and there was none to help.

13 Then they cried unto the Lord in their trouble, and he saved them out of their distresses.

14 He brought them out of darkness and the shadow of death, and brake their bands in sunder.

15 Oh that men would praise the Lord for his goodness, and for his wonderful works to the children of men!

16 For he hath broken the gates of brass, and cut the bars of iron in sunder.

17 Fools because of their transgression, and because of their iniquities, are afflicted.

18 Their soul abhorreth all manner of meat; and they draw near unto the gates of death.

19 Then they cry unto the Lord in their trouble, and he saveth them out of their distresses.

20 He sent his word, and healed them, and delivered them from their destructions.

21 Oh that men would praise the Lord for his goodness, and for his wonderful works to the children of men!

22 And let them sacrifice the sacrifices of thanksgiving, and declare his works with rejoicing.

23 They that go down to the sea in ships, that do business in great waters;

24 These see the works of the Lord, and his wonders in the deep.

25 For he commandeth, and raiseth the stormy wind, which lifteth up the waves thereof.

26 They mount up to the heaven, they go down again to the depths: their soul is melted because of trouble.

27 They reel to and fro, and stagger like a drunken man, and are at their wit's end.

28 Then they cry unto the Lord in their trouble, and he bringeth them out of their distresses.

29 He maketh the storm a calm, so that the waves thereof are still.

30 Then are they glad because they be quiet; so he bringeth them unto their desired haven.

31 Oh that men would praise the Lord for his goodness, and for his wonderful works to the children of men!

32 Let them exalt him also in the congregation of the people, and praise him in the assembly of the elders.

33 He turneth rivers into a wilderness, and the watersprings into dry ground;

34 A fruitful land into barrenness, for the wickedness of them that dwell therein.

35 He turneth the wilderness into a standing water, and dry ground into watersprings.

36 And there he maketh the hungry to dwell, that they may prepare a city for habitation;

37 And sow the fields, and plant vineyards, which may yield fruits of increase.

38 He blesseth them also, so that they are multiplied greatly; and suffereth not their cattle to decrease.

39 Again, they are minished and brought low through oppression, affliction, and sorrow.

40 He poureth contempt upon princes, and causeth them to wander in the wilderness, where there is no way.

41 Yet setteth he the poor on high from affliction, and maketh him families like a flock.

42 The righteous shall see it, and rejoice: and all iniquity shall stop her mouth.

43 Whoso is wise, and will observe these things, even they shall understand the lovingkindness of the Lord.

108:1 O God, my heart is fixed; I will sing and give praise, even with my glory.

2 Awake, psaltery and harp: I myself will awake early.

3 I will praise thee, O Lord, among the people: and I will sing praises unto thee among the nations.

4 For thy mercy is great above the heavens: and thy truth reacheth unto the clouds.

5 Be thou exalted, O God, above the heavens: and thy glory above all the earth;

6 That thy beloved may be delivered: save with thy right hand, and answer me.

7 God hath spoken in his holiness; I will rejoice, I will divide Shechem, and mete out the valley of Succoth.

8 Gilead is mine; Manasseh is mine; Ephraim also is the strength of mine head; Judah is my lawgiver;

9 Moab is my washpot; over Edom will I cast out my shoe; over Philistia will I triumph.

10 Who will bring me into the strong city? who will lead me into Edom?

11 Wilt not thou, O God, who hast cast us off? and wilt not thou, O God, go forth with our hosts?

12 Give us help from trouble: for vain is the help of man.

13 Through God we shall do valiantly: for he it is that shall tread down our enemies.

109:1 Hold not thy peace, O God of my praise;

2 For the mouth of the wicked and the mouth of the deceitful are opened against me: they have spoken against me with a lying tongue.

3 They compassed me about also with words of hatred; and fought against me without a cause.

4 For my love they are my adversaries: but I give myself unto prayer.

5 And they have rewarded me evil for good, and hatred for my love.

6 Set thou a wicked man over him: and let Satan stand at his right hand.

7 When he shall be judged, let him be condemned: and let his prayer become sin.

8 Let his days be few; and let another take his office.

9 Let his children be fatherless, and his wife a widow.

10 Let his children be continually vagabonds, and beg: let them seek their bread also out of their desolate places.

11 Let the extortioner catch all that he hath; and let the strangers spoil his labour.

12 Let there be none to extend mercy unto him: neither let there be any to favour his fatherless children.

13 Let his posterity be cut off; and in the generation following let their name be blotted out.

14 Let the iniquity of his fathers be remembered with the Lord; and let not the sin of his mother be blotted out.

15 Let them be before the Lord continually, that he may cut off the memory of them from the earth.

16 Because that he remembered not to shew mercy, but persecuted the poor and needy man, that he might even slay the broken in heart.

17 As he loved cursing, so let it come unto him: as he delighted not in blessing, so let it be far from him.

18 As he clothed himself with cursing like as with his garment, so let it come into his bowels like water, and like oil into his bones.

19 Let it be unto him as the garment which covereth him, and for a girdle wherewith he is girded continually.

20 Let this be the reward of mine adversaries from the Lord, and of them that speak evil against my soul.

21 But do thou for me, O God the Lord, for thy name's sake: because thy mercy is good, deliver thou me.

22 For I am poor and needy, and my heart is wounded within me.

23 I am gone like the shadow when it declineth: I am tossed up and down as the locust.

24 My knees are weak through fasting; and my flesh faileth of fatness.

25 I became also a reproach unto them: when they looked upon me they shaked their heads.

26 Help me, O Lord my God: O save me according to thy mercy:

27 That they may know that this is thy hand; that thou, Lord, hast done it.

28 Let them curse, but bless thou: when they arise, let them be ashamed; but let thy servant rejoice.

29 Let mine adversaries be clothed with shame, and let them cover themselves with their own confusion, as with a mantle.

30 I will greatly praise the Lord with my mouth; yea, I will praise him among the multitude.

31 For he shall stand at the right hand of the poor, to save him from those that condemn his soul.

You don't have to be perfect to do God's work. God's creation offers an opportunity to try to understand God's intentions and how He looks at and sees the variables that exist within the different individuals that has grown from His creation. Not one of us are perfect, but God accepts that. He actually uses our differences to accomplish what His plans are.

God's desire to fill His Heavens gives us the opportunity to repent and enter His Kingdom. Even until the end of time. Clear to the end of the millennium while Christ rules the New Earth for a thousand years. God's love is that strong. God is love.

 hapter 5

Grouping

THE LORD ARRANGES A VARIETY IN GROUPS. HE HAS GROUPINGS in all of the world. He mixes good and bad, big and strong, beautiful and ugly, both in looks and in actions. He has His groups with different ways of worship and beliefs.

God mixes Satan and believers. He wants us to individually recognize Him and what He expects from them. The presence of evil is accepted by some. The acceptance of Godliness by many of us, but by different ways. The countries of the world are filled with the groupings. Disagreements are prevalent. God lets that happen. Misconduct and fighting exists in all groups. The continents are filled with different groups and attitudes. Some God likes, some He does not, but His love and caring are also always present and wanting everyone to have a chance to come to our gracious and forgiving Lord.

Within the continents and countries that make them up cause the conflicts and accomplishments from different groups. Sometimes the groups can work together or at least tolerate each other. Sometimes not! The Middle East has been in conflict for thousands of years, and that is where God sent His Son, Jesus, to give the love of forgiveness of original sin and open the doors to Heaven. But the conflicts of the Arabs and Christians still have conflict over land and power. Those groups' attitudes will only be changed by the end of times. God is disappointed by this but is totally aware of the fact that nothing is going to change. God could change anything or eliminate whatever is wrong, but that is not His plan presently.

Within those countries of the world are segments of rule. In the U.S. it is states, in some countries it is kingdoms, in some it is tribes or ethnic groups. In some, there are monarchies. Different groups, but as stated there are different groups by other distinctions. The emotions of those people and groups in different geographies is still a mixture. Any little or large difference is often the cause of rash or obstructive behavior. God or faith is often pushed aside to expose true feelings and resentments.

These groups go farther than countries. Counties in states or provinces also contain groups of different thoughts and beliefs. Cities, towns, and villages all have power struggles and disagreements. Neighborhoods and rural areas all have groupings. Good and bad live within. It is the people that create or change the attitudes toward one another.

It is hard for me, and I am sure for God, to understand why the races and ethnic groups cannot find a way to exist together in harmony. If your father and mother, brothers and sisters, and relatives can have disagreements, but settle them by forgiving and letting bygones be bygones. Those disagreements can be serious, and some offenses repeated, but eventually love overcomes them and reconciliation will happen. Usually both sides are happy about this.

In World War II, we in the U.S. hated the Japanese and the Germans. They were brutal and imposed terrible suffering and torture causing death, scars, starving, beaten, and forced to be exposed to dismal conditions. They were not kind to their prisoners and did not follow God's teachings. Only hate prevailed.

In many wars and battles, it was unbearable for many. Now 70 plus years later, the animosity toward Germans and Japanese has been put aside and they are allies.

Think about this in the context of blacks and Caucasians, Asians and Muslims, race against race. What feeds the prejudice and hate and resentment toward one another? Is it just for personal benefits for your skin color? Expecting to be different and superior because of how you were born. (God didn't want it to be this way!)

Do we try to make ourselves stand out, be different looking, making your resentment show by strutting around wearing our clothes that are different than most people do? Using our hair, whiskers, tattoos, and physical appearance to set you out different, saying, "I'm not a conformant to society. I'm different and I deserve something because I'm different. I don't want to be like you, and I'm entitled to something because of something that happened 200 years ago." (God excels in love.)

Oh yes, there will always be those individuals and groups who will carry the torch of hatred who are led by Satan because (hatred is the basis of evil). <u>Evil drives people apart because it undermines God</u>! The presence of evil is everywhere. In our governments, in U.S. and around the world is overrun by hatred because <u>that is what Satan wants</u>.

We can solve this only through God, but most countries say they can become powerful and be invincible. This is wrong. Since the beginning of time, there is example after example of God's will and power can make any country be defeated and overthrown if they ignore God's help.

It is the same with individuals. We can be accepted as equals if we show our love of God and love our neighbors as we love ourselves. We cannot carry a grudge and a chip on our shoulders and show hatred if we want to make our lives peaceful. Ignore the bigots, they are evil.

(Lead us not into temptation but deliver us from evil.)

Present yourself, your surroundings, and your character in a positive way, whether you are rich or poor. Treat everyone equal no matter what they look like, act like, or dress like you. You can make your appearance however you want, but the perception of you as a person has to show your caring and loving nature. If you really have love in your heart, even if you are God's servant, preacher, evangelist, or regular person, your true heart and love will not show if it is not sincere and free of prejudice.

If we can forget and forgive what happened in World War II, we can overcome ethnic bias.

No one is or has been a slave like before the Civil War, but many of us are slaves because were subject to the government's slavery by expecting or getting taken care of with government entitlements. Now! I am a big supporter of charity, helping those less fortunate who are unable to help themselves, but there are jobs available if you want to work. It is easy to make excuses, procrastinate, or be lazy, but just so you know, it is not only self-gratification and pride to accomplish, but it keeps resentment from others who do work, and keeps prejudice away.

You may say, "What do I know about racism?" Well, my great grandmother, 100% Cherokee Native American, was on the Trail of Tears from the Carolinas to Oklahoma.

We did not go around playing the race card, we tried to blend into society when I was a little boy. We, as a family of seven children, grew up close to the Reservation, but a lot of our family and relatives are Indian mixed with other nationalities.

I know persecution because I saw it, just as I saw it in the southern states when I worked in the south. I saw the conditions the African Americans lived under. I saw the lack of opportunities. Some of my black friends with college degrees did not know if they could find jobs to match their educations. I felt bad for them. Even today, I think of that and I am glad to see opportunity for all of us. "Praise the Lord." So you see, things and conditions have changed. Oh, there are still some that have hatred and hate-mongers, but they are few. They can still gather in gangs or groups to expound their hate and injuries or kill God's people, but most of them want to be recognized or feared, steal or cheat, or gain wealth and power. They are driven by Satan. They have become evil or mislead. They do not think about tomorrow when they face their judgement after death. Life is fragile and is not a long period of time. Life flies by fast. You are going to face death and its consequences sooner than you think!

When you are young, you don't believe that life is short, you may think you are 10-foot-tall and can handle anything that comes to you. You do not understand God or His plans. God's plans from your beginning was to have you in His Kingdom, but He expects you to prepare for His Kingdom.

Many people do not show their faith or comment to God until they get older and realize that they are not following the Lord's wishes for their redemption.

God did not create us and then go away and let us determine our course! He watches our course, He never left or never will.

He observes us every minute and every day of our lives. He sees your victories and He sees your defeats. He sees your sadness and He sees your joy. He can influence all those things and He gives His love to you but leaves it up to you to overcome or take care of those situations yourself. He gave you free will, and He gave you the ability to turn to Him to get through those events that are part of your life.

Unusual things can happen. Loss of a loved one. Physical conditions from disease, accidents, impairments of health or stress of living conditions. Being poor, homeless, abuse in your surroundings, all factors of life can be your change in your life, and they can change you. Your attitude and personality can change. You may wonder why God lets these things happen and you may resent God or take Him out of your life. He will never take you out of His love for you.

Pain, disappointments, loss of wealth, your job or your belongings are a part of life. God lets it happen and leave you to change it. God will help if you turn to Him, but it will be in His time, when He is ready.

His chosen people were put in bondage, slavery and banished to another land; but He eventually saved them. That saving was once 40 years, and the other 70 years.

Pain can be a cleansing. Jesus took unbelievable, almost unimaginable pain in His crucifixion. Why? He was cleaning the sins of all people for thousands of years.

Let's talk about us, God's people. Our emotions, dreams of success, greed and lust are sometimes driving us to sin. Sex, money, power, position, fame, recognition, envy, jealousy, pride, selfishness, resentment, hate, superiority, bullying, devious actions, cheating, stealing, robbing, burglarizing, demanding space, taking advantage, unkindness, not charitable, not helping others when we could, generosity to charities, giving up your time to support a need or a fundraiser, going to join others in worshiping. Putting yourself first in group activities for pleasure. Dishonest in discussion, untruthful answers, or comments. Embellishing things you have done to impress others. Making yourself more than you are in you are better than others. Looking down on less fortunate or weaker and feeling superior can lead to a big let-down when the truth comes out. "God is watching."

These are common sins of all of us. Being humble and caring are more in God's desires.

I feel sorry for God, and I feel sorry for the U.S. if God decides He's given us enough warnings and we are not listening. In 800 years or so BC, God put the Israelites in bondage, slavery for 40 years. He allowed the Assyrians to defeat Israel. What if He decides to let us be defeated and overcome our nation? Don't think it couldn't happen. It can happen without a major war. We can become a communist nation just by our government ignoring God and letting us become so overcome by entitlements and socialism that we are not able to carry that load of giveaway programs that cause dependency on the government to support us. Where people don't work and depend on others to pay for their existence. That will take away the incentive to work, stop the desire to excel to get ahead financially. Entrepreneur opportunity to create new companies and jobs.

Why work when someone else (government) will support you. Reward you to have kids and welfare. The trend that those on welfare raise their kids to also depend on the government.

Soon the revenue from taxing others isn't enough to meet the demand to keep the county from bankruptcy.

We humans can find it so easy to succumb to personal desires and pleasures. In the workplace, our neighborhoods, when working out at the gym or YMCA. Any activity that exposes us in close contact to the opposite sex or individuals with ideas that are sinful can cause us to weaken to sin. Desire to be rich or powerful can lead you to sin or at least consider it. Temptation is always close by. Procrastination or making up a reason why it would be okay to sin. If your daily life is difficult or filled with disappointment or dissatisfaction, you are weakened to temptation. Looking for a little excitement or personal pleasure makes it hard to turn down a sinful action. We all are sinners, because of free will, but sin never comes without punishment or worry if you do give in to sin.

Getting caught in doing sin can be devastating to your life. God sometimes will not interfere, because He knows that the sin will come out eventually, and your suffering will happen when the sin comes to surface, or your conscience will punish you.

It's tough to go through life and not sin in some fashion. The only way not to sin is to stay in close touch with God through His Holy Spirit and ask for strength and wisdom.

We can be faced with a sinful situation and that is when we need the faith and mentality to avoid it! We are human, and have free will, and it is easy to find an excuse to have a chance to enjoy the moment. What is the result? Well, you may feel a pleasure for a time and think God will forgive you, and He will, but it does leave a scar. A scar that will have to be accounted for at some time later.

God knows that those things will happen and yes, you can be forgiven, but in your journey through life, those scars will shine out and cause your breaking your faith will shine out like the strongest light in the night.

God cleanses us with pain and afflictions. When we are sick or hurt, or suffering in any way, it may be that you are going through a cleansing of your sins!! Your sickness or affliction may be related to your sins of now and in the past.

Jesus' crucifixion did not have to be that severe. God could have let His Son, Jesus, die for our sins in a less severe and brutal way. The pain and torturing of our Savior was far and above the ability of a normal human being could endure. Jesus lost all of His blood during the punishment. He was beaten and whipped, and they still had to put a spear in His side for death.

God could have intervened, but the pain had to be cleansing enough to forgive thousands of years and millions and millions of people from original sin. The Holy Spirit was witnessing, and God was witnessing the punishment!

How difficult for God to witness His Son being abused! How hard to watch … when it finally ended, God showed His remorse and love of His Son and what Jesus had done.

I feel sorry for God. I really feel sorry for Him to witness the crucifixion and all the evil, and sinning, and turmoil going on in the past and in present day. This is not what God expected.

The evil that has covered the world since creation was, and is, the undermining of God's will. The existence of Satan's demons and followers are a constant strain on God's people. The evidence of evil is so prominent in today's times. Hate and revenge and destruction of one people against other people is causing more and more reason to know that it is time to get close to our Creator.

We have insanity in our societies that can be swayed to do evil things to innocent people. Killings, crippling, tearing into the bodies of God's human race. Bodies that God made and them causing injuries and deaths. Wars and terrorism are rampant. No concern for life or health. Life, no matter how innocent is exempt from those evil forces. God's people being considered expendable are not accepted by our Father!

Stealing, robbery, taking by force is not what we are expected to do! How depressing it must be for God's nature for caring. He wanted mankind to have a loving nature, like His.

God intended for our lives and conditions of life to be more pleasant for all, and not for just the ones of us that are fortunate to have the pleasures of a good life.

Why is it that some of us have it better than others? God works in mysterious ways. Those ways may seem fair or unfair, but He had His plan. We are all placed in a position of life. We have no control as to whom we are born to as our parents. We have no control over the conditions we are born into as far as wealth, safety, or environment. We have no control over what genes or chromosomes or body composure will be. The constant is that we are born, and the results are what they are!

Some of us will beat the odds of their situation and improve it or some of us will accept what it is and live it.

Others of us will be determined and buck the odds and through circumstance, luck, hard work ethic, and determination will improve their condition. Integrity, commitment, and perseverance can get you some of the way, but God can help you! "You cannot out give the Lord." Effort or giving of help to others on your way can and will be returned to you in some way.

Doing without luxury and saving for a nest egg to start a business or an opportunity to invest in a safe investment.

I know of a young man who was struggling to support his family. A wife expecting their second child and doing okay, but budget was tight. He would take any extra hours to help their financial needs. Over the next few years, he saved $2,800. He took that and got a loan for $5,000 and started his first business that he could work in his off-job hours. That business was making a little money. Never taking any earnings but putting it back to expand his business. His family lived off his job wages. The business grew. He continued with his family to live modestly. One year when he was still getting established, he decided he hadn't tithed as much as he should have according to him, so he went to the bank and borrowed an amount he wanted to give to his church. The banker asked what the loan was for and he told the truth, tithing. The bank gave him the loan and he gave it to the church. Within 90 days his regular job, which was in commission selling, had a big sale and more than paid off the loan.

You can't out give the Lord!

That lesson still lives today for that man.

The Lord wants us to know that whatever you are born into, no matter what the circumstances are, and no matter how few opportunities or how depressed you circumstances are, you should always be trying and looking for ways to improve your status. You may never succeed, but God wants you to try!

Not just monetarily but mentally as well. Happiness is not about wealth or money; it is peace and happiness. It is appreciating what you have, and what God has planned for you. Those who forget to be thankful will (may) find themselves bitter and defeated and find self-pity for their existence.

I feel sorry for those who accept status quo and fail to try to do better. Never give up! God never gives up on you! Praise the Lord and you will see. There is always a chance through God. He expects you to try to be better: hard work, integrity, ingenuity, creativity, and always willing to do extra.

I don't know why God has made different situations for

different people. Luxury or poverty, opportunity or bondage, royalty or slavery, easy work, or hard work, educated or illiterate, opportunity or no opportunity. Born to wealthy family or born to less fortunate. That is what we are dealt when we come into this world. Whatever our circumstances, we must be looking for a way to be better. Rise up and make the effort! Get to be noticed and a good example to your associates and leaders or bosses. Do not be afraid to ask for opportunity! Just remember everything comes from God. Ask Him to help you while you show that you are capable of learning and committed to success. (Success is measured in the heart) not just in wealth or earnings. Show your giving side to help others when you're in a position to do so.

Never give up. It is always in God's hands, and always in God's time. God is present even in the worse place or the worse conditions.

Ethnic people who conform to environment are accepted for all.

Have you ever noticed that the racial reaction is always absent when the ethnic person appears in the same look and behavior as those around them? A person in clothes and appearance is the same as those around them or their dress code is presentable to the crowd? Oh, there are still bigots out there, but those will be disrupted when they find themselves in the minority. Of course, your attitude if you're self-centered, act superior, or over-bearing, then you will be rejected by mostly everybody regardless of your race.

I feel sorry for God to see such a small percentage of His people disrupting all of society. Jackie Robinson did what he did for baseball by ignoring abuse and proving his point by his performance. God expects us to forgive, ignore, and prove ourselves by example. You abuse me, but I forgave you! That will cast guilt on the offenders. That guilt will expand to others who are offensive, and God's love will live within you!!!

Don't you see ... God is love! Love is more powerful than hate! It is hard not to like someone who likes you and admires you. Plus, the Holy Spirit is there as a witness. God sees from the Holy Spirit. "The love of Jesus is the door to Heaven." So we see another parallel. The parallel of God's creation from beginning to end. The prophets from Elijah, to all the prophets, to Moses, the recipient of the commandments. When Elijah and Moses appeared to Jesus on the mount, representing the laws was Moses, and Elijah representing the prophets in the presence of Peter, James, and John, it frightened all three of them, but it fulfilled a prophesy.

In the story of God's creation, we find the parallel of God's intensions, with the sin, disobedience, and rejection of God and the variables of human nature. Mankind is unpredictable even in the greatest devotion of God's Word. I'm sorry Lord, that we can be so erratic.

As difficult as it was to get the pharaoh to release the Israelites from 40 years of bondage, and all You had to do to prove Your power to convince him to let Moses lead Your people out of Egypt and how resistant he was.

That is somewhat paralleled in mankind today. You give us so many chances to see what You can and will do for us, and many of us cannot see the way to get Your love and care You offer. I'm sorry we make it so difficult to "heed" Your Word.

I am totally in awe as I study Your scripture and try to understand more about You. My dreams and visions help me understand and realize what disappointment we put You through. What a totally wonderful Lord You are to forgive us our sins, and how difficult it is for us to follow through the temptations and evil that lures us in human emotions and how You understand and forgive us, and we forgive those who treat us wrong and unjustly. Being like You and love our neighbors is so comforting when we can do that! It is hard to really let go and turn everything over to You, Lord. But once we do: (How Great Thou Art).

God has provided the information about the end of times which I pointed out on the parallels of God's intentions at the creation of man to the end of times. To fill His Heavens with believers and true followers of God's Trinity. Starting in Daniel, we get information about the end of times. I feel sorry for those who do not believe. I feel sorry for God when the non-believers are refusing to understand God's will and intensions for us.

God gives us prophetic vison of reality. In Revelation and the book of Daniel will refer to the tribulations and the rapture – assuring that God's wrath will not fall on the believers and faithful. It also opens the door as to speculation about the timeframe of the tribulations and when the rapture will occur. I believe the rapture is after the start of the first tribulation. I also believe the length of the tribulation is not specific.

When God starts the process of the end will depend on what God sees what's happening in His Creation. If there is a need for extra or limited time to redeem more followers, He will re-arrange His timeframe. I feel sorry for God that He is restricted on some of His due process, but humans are so unpredictable.

God is watching the earth and His children so that we continue to have the opportunity to repent. Sometimes I think God thinks He's herding cats ...

We have caused God many variations of what His children are becoming. There is so much turmoil, with hate and greed and violence and pride and power sought, and prejudice, and superiority. The egos and controlling minds trying to convert others to their beliefs. Willing to kill, conquer, force their agenda. Don't you feel sorry for God to deal with all this?

The Holy Spirit is God's calvary as I've said before as a believer of Jesus (Romans 8:29 and Thessalonians 2:13, and again in Galatians 4:19, all KJV) we are accepted and gifted with the Spirit of God. These gifts of the Holy Spirit we must be good purveyors of God's words and Jesus' promises. We become disciples and give our efforts and actions to bring others into God's family of believers and worshipers. Our rewards for bringing more souls to fill the Heavens as God's parallel is intended.

God measures us and studies us to see how He might use us. Are we listening? Do we seek righteousness? Psalms denotes what is right in righteousness. In KJV Psalms 4:5, 23:3, 52:3, 111, 112. It's grounded in the character of God's intentions. God expects the righteous to be in His place! Many sins can eliminate righteousness.

Freedom, good health, low stress, and no suffering are blessings, praise the Lord! If some of these or even one of these is missing, you may be getting a cleansing from God. That cleansing could lead to salvation.

A community of people or a gathering of people can create a fellowship that helps to sustain your faith and help with your burdens and give you discipline in your focus of God. Sharing thoughts, prayers, and unify you with fellow Christians and communion with God.

God uses us and picks each of us for whatever He wants to accomplish. Even if we're sinful, He may still use us.

My objective for this book is to make you realize that God is right beside you and His Holy Spirit is with Him. You cannot think that God is a long way off and you'll get to Him later. It doesn't work like that!!! He is here. He knows us, who and what we are.

All the pleasures of sin only last a short time and the thrill is when Satan sees you as a possible follower of him. Many sins you enjoy, but you won't even remember what they gave you. Many of those sins will haunt you for years.

Get your head straight! Know that your God is real and loving. How you hurt Him when He only wants the best for you. He watches you like He did Adam and Eve, and how He gave them everything in luxury and as soon as they were alone, they turned to Satan for a temptation of a different experience. Adam and Eve sacrificed a life in Paradise for a little adventure.

In our lives, we wish we could go back to our sins and eliminate them. God feels the same way on some of the people He entrusted for obedience.

Just please accept the fact that God is always present, and you are seen in whatever your actions and activities are. Think about what you do, realizing that God is watching us and all the people alive and dead.

The Holy Spirit is so powerful that there is no place you can hide from God. Ask Jonah! God controls everything. His actions are in His time, but scripture tells us God will punish, God will control your environment, weather, praise, choose you to do His work and expect obedience, but God will always love you even if He loses you to Satan.

# Chapter 6

Wisdom

Some consider this the greatest of all blessings. The most wealthy man that lived was Solomon, son of David. When the Lord asked Solomon what he desired, Solomon asked for wisdom. Not wealth, material items as land or other assets. The gift of knowledge and wisdom brought the wealth in the addition to the intelligence.

Wisdom can also give us the ability to understand others and know when to speak and not speak, when to give advice and when not to! Knowing when to listen more and comment less will also give us the opportunity to learn from others. The art of analysis and understanding allows us wisdom to serve us in hearing and consider what we're listening to and give full attention to other viewpoints and opinions.

We can gain more wisdom by being aware of others' knowledge! Learning to listen to others will allow you the opportunity to learn more and retain the will to learn more. Never feel like you know it all about anything. There is always more knowledge out there and you can learn from those in lower positions that may have no authority or looked at for knowledge but through experience they do have wisdom.

Deuteronomy 7:6 (KJV) "For thou art an holy people unto the Lord thy God: the Lord thy God hath chosen thee to be a special people unto himself, above all people that are upon the face of the earth." You are His people ... His treasured possession!!!

The extent of God's love is unexplainable. He loves us in ways we cannot fathom. Jeremiah 31:3, Romans 5:38, 8:35, and 38:39 (KJV).

Even when we offend our Lord and become unworthy to receive God's love, He never gave up on us, and leaves the opportunity for repentance and returning to His grace. The greatest of all emotions is the love that fills our hearts from the praises of God's love for us, His children! Forgiveness dwells in the hearts of those worthy.

A salvation in itself is what we have in hope. No matter how dire our situation and discouraged we become, the element of hope is always present and that gives us the fortitude to continue on because God gives us hope for and encouragement that all is not lost, and our dreams for a better tomorrow and future are out there.

Our loving God engages us intimately with His love, He is pained by our sins and by those we rebel against Him.

His love overcomes all obstacles if we atone for our inequities and repent and love Him back with our whole heart!!

The good news is that the same God who empowered Nehemiah to rebuild the Temple in Jerusalem over 2000 years ago is there for us today. If you will only ask for His help and be sincere!

Psalm 50:15 (KJV) "And call upon me in the day of trouble: I will deliver thee, and thou shalt glorify me."

Jude 1:1-25 (KJV, my takeaway from scriptures) "1 Jude, the servant of Jesus Christ, and brother of James, to them that are sanctified by God the Father, and preserved in Jesus Christ, and called: 2 Mercy unto you, and peace, and love, be multiplied.

3 Beloved, when I gave all diligence to write unto you of the common salvation, it was needful for me to write unto you, and exhort you that ye should earnestly contend for the faith which was once delivered unto the saints.

4 For there are certain men crept in unawares, who were before of old ordained to this condemnation, ungodly men, turning the grace of our God into lasciviousness, and denying the only Lord God, and our Lord Jesus Christ.

5 I will therefore put you in remembrance, though ye once knew this, how that the Lord, having saved the people out of the land of Egypt, afterward destroyed them that believed not.

6 And the angels which kept not their first estate, but left their own habitation, he hath reserved in everlasting chains under darkness unto the judgment of the great day.

7 Even as Sodom and Gomorrha, and the cities about them in like manner, giving themselves over to fornication, and going after strange flesh, are set forth for an example, suffering the vengeance of eternal fire.

8 Likewise also these filthy dreamers defile the flesh, despise dominion, and speak evil of dignities.

9 Yet Michael the archangel, when contending with the devil he disputed about the body of Moses, durst not bring against him a railing accusation, but said, The Lord rebuke thee.

10 But these speak evil of those things which they know not:

but what they know naturally, as brute beasts, in those things they corrupt themselves.

11 Woe unto them! for they have gone in the way of Cain, and ran greedily after the error of Balaam for reward, and perished in the gainsaying of Core.

12 These are spots in your feasts of charity, when they feast with you, feeding themselves without fear: clouds they are without water, carried about of winds; trees whose fruit withereth, without fruit, twice dead, plucked up by the roots;

13 Raging waves of the sea, foaming out their own shame; wandering stars, to whom is reserved the blackness of darkness for ever.

14 And Enoch also, the seventh from Adam, prophesied of these, saying, Behold, the Lord cometh with ten thousands of his saints,

15 To execute judgment upon all, and to convince all that are ungodly among them of all their ungodly deeds which they have ungodly committed, and of all their hard speeches which ungodly sinners have spoken against him.

16 These are murmurers, complainers, walking after their own lusts; and their mouth speaketh great swelling words, having men's persons in admiration because of advantage.

17 But, beloved, remember ye the words which were spoken before of the apostles of our Lord Jesus Christ;

18 How that they told you there should be mockers in the last time, who should walk after their own ungodly lusts.

19 These be they who separate themselves, sensual, having not the Spirit.

20 But ye, beloved, building up yourselves on your most holy faith, praying in the Holy Ghost,

21 Keep yourselves in the love of God, looking for the mercy of our Lord Jesus Christ unto eternal life.

22 And of some have compassion, making a difference:

23 And others save with fear, pulling them out of the fire; hating even the garment spotted by the flesh.

24 Now unto him that is able to keep you from falling, and to present you faultless before the presence of his glory with exceeding joy,

25 To the only wise God our Saviour, be glory and majesty, dominion and power, both now and ever. Amen.

You will notice, people will shy away from someone talking spirituality. Someone talking about God or Jesus or the Holy Spirit.

The reason can be guilt, avoiding who they consider the person a zealot, or preaching, or holier-then-thou. They do not want to hear it because they do not want to change their ways or lose the thrill or enjoyment of sin. They may feel guilty or do not want their friend to think they are religious. They are not worried about the hereafter or life beyond death.

This book is meant to reach those who have not committed to having a relationship with God, or Best Friend (at least He wants to be).

It is easier to yield to temptation and allowing Satan to rule their lives. If they could see the peace and tranquility in a Christian's eyes and realize how much comfort they have, when God is a priority in their lives. Love and lust are four letter words but have such different results!

The Holy Spirit is so much more than we realize ... as with the apostles, God knew the Holy Spirit would be with them to spread the "Good News," Christ's promises. So, with the Holy Spirit, God has the Calvary to give through God your daily being! Pray that you always are aware of the presence of God's Spirit. God knows us! Our strengths, our weaknesses, our hope and desires, but most of all, our needs!!!!!

1 Timothy 6:6-16 (KJV) 6 But godliness with contentment is great gain. 7 For we brought nothing into this world, and it is certain we can carry nothing out. 8 And having food and raiment let us be therewith content. 9 But they that will be rich fall into temptation and a snare, and into many foolish and hurtful lusts, which drown men in destruction and perdition. 10 For the love of money is the root of all evil: which while some coveted after, they have erred from the faith, and pierced themselves through with many sorrows. 11 But thou, O man of God, flee these things; and follow after righteousness, godliness, faith, love, patience, meekness. 12 Fight the good fight of faith, lay hold on eternal life, whereunto thou art also called, and hast professed a good profession before many witnesses. 13 I give thee charge in the sight of God, who quickeneth all things, and before Christ Jesus, who before Pontius Pilate witnessed a good confession; 14 That thou keep this commandment without spot, unrebukable, until the appearing of our Lord Jesus Christ: 15 Which in his times he shall shew, who is the blessed and only Potentate, the King of kings, and Lord of lords; 16 Who only hath immortality, dwelling in the light which no man can approach unto; whom no man hath seen, nor can see: to whom be honour and power everlasting. Amen.

 hapter 7

My Good Friend, God, is always there for me. My good friend and I talk every day. He loves me when I am bad, and He loves me when I am good. When we talk, I ask him how He is doing. He does not answer me with words, but He lets me know in dreams and visions.

He is never away from me to hear me. What a great friend He is! I complain and ask for favors and He hears my every word. I do not always get the response I want, but I know He has got my best interests in His heart.

I do not have to use fancy words or make an eloquent statement. He just wants to be treated like any of my other friends. I really lucked out to find His friendship. He does not expect me to give Him anything but love and respect and obey His commandments. He forgives me for offending Him over and over. What other friend would continue to accept you if you conducted yourself in an offensive way to their expectations?

I get so much satisfaction knowing that I can put my friend, God, in control of all my problems and needs.

I know my friend smiles when I put my trust in Him. I smile

when I think about what my friend has done for me! Not only that, but my friend has made an offer to me that I can come and live with Him when I leave my earthly home.

Satan's mission to undermine God is to divide us against each other. Satan uses racial bias, wealth bias, expectation of someone else to do the work and give us part of what they make to make the opportunity to be lazy or give them a good life. If we choose to be different, then we do not fit in with society. We're racists.

If we want to solve social differences like racism, or prejudice, "then look in the mirror!!" Matthew 6:14-15 (KJV) says, "For if ye forgive men their trespasses, your Heavenly Father will also forgive you: but if ye forgive not men their trespasses, neither will your Father forgive your trespasses."

If you carry grudges form the past, forgive! We know they were wrong and abusive, but God says forgive! If you do not forgive, you cannot be forgiven. If abuse exists today, consider that Satan is causing it! Those who are offensive are not worth the time to hate and want revenge. They are doing Satan's work. Conform to your society and you will be accepted. God will eventually step in and correct the situation.

Jackie Robinson took abuse and rejection to overcome the bias and stupidity as a gentleman. He opened the door for minorities and narrow-minded racists, and now some of our most respected citizens are athletes. Same in politics, businesses, and other fields! These people could help with getting rid of hatred, but some of them make things worse, because they stir the hatred publicly.

Look in the mirror again and ask yourself: am I part of the problem, or am I trying to help stamp out racism? Looking different and acting different are not the answer.

Forgive or you will not be forgiven. (Matthew 6:14-15 KJV again.)

It is tough to forgive when you use your bias to support your status in life. Going out on a limb and speculating and belief. Controversy and disagreement will react to this, our understanding of the possibility.

"Pain is God's way of healing our sins." He allows pain for cleansing the sins of people. Today's protestors show the shame of exposure and resentment and persecution by so many people supporting the destruction of God's country. The brutality is extreme because that's more sins, the greater the division of God's love.

Cleansing is a warning of purification or overcoming the sins that weigh on the soul.

Purification of our sins opens the doors for being worthy of God's love. Some people may suffer from pain in a purification and get no good from it at all, because they do not turn to God or look for redemption. Suffering does not lead to cleansing unless you turn to God for relief or gratitude for cleansing you to have the opportunity to join The Kingdom!

Paul, a beloved servant of God was not a good man before he committed to God through Jesus. This is a good example of healing. Bitten by a snake in the desert with treatment unavailable would be very painful. The swelling and pain would be unbearable. Being shipwrecked would be a psychological and mental pain as well as caring about being rescued. It would give Paul lots of time to meditate and pray. God was cleansing Paul, who went on to be one of the most prolific writers of God's scriptures. David, who God loved dearly and one of God's greatest warriors was not perfect, but he loved his Father in Heaven. He was not given the chance to build God's temple because he was not totally cleansed.

This theory and belief that God heals through pain is not accepted by all followers. I am sure, but there is a cleansing process for us, as is mentioned in scripture!

Confession and God's forgiveness is real, but there are consequences to healing. Sometimes just getting resolution is not the entire consequence. Especially if you keep repeating the offenses to our Father.

You can thank God for going through discomfort. We should give thanks for the cleansing.

Sometimes God is warning us when He gives us clues or warnings. He gave the Israelites warning after warning that they would be punished if they did not quit their rejection of God's law. He warned them by sending the Assyrians (the first Terrorists) into battle with the Israelites. God allowed the Israelites to repel them at first. When the Israelites did not change, He let the Assyrians conquer them and put them into bondage for 40 years and destroy their temple. Slaves in Egypt for 40 years ... God's favorite people put in bondage for all that time. Later we learn that the Israelites disobeyed God's law and the Babylonians defeated them and again they were in bondage for 70 years. God's favorite people!

What about the present? The United States was created under God and Christians. Are we being warned? I think so. When the World Trade Center's towers were destroyed, it was by terrorists like the Assyrians. The embassies and our ship being bombed and attacked. Warnings?

When the nations say they are going to prepare for future attacks and become impregnable. Become stronger militarily and protect ourselves. They think they can take care of themselves. They are still not asking God to help them ... big mistake! There has never been a battle won or a war won by anyone that God didn't want them to win!!!

God is in control of all things and if He is not on our side and in our hearts, we cannot do it on our own!!!

No matter how strong or talented we are, it is still God that gave you that ability or accomplishment and we had better get that imbedded in our minds. Celebrities who think they are special because God gave them special talents in sports, entertainment, business, or statis. God's gift, but their ego is so big they think they can support their opinions and influence others. Well think again you egotists. You only influence those who already had agreed with you! You're no better than the street vendor when you divide our country, cause bigotry, and forget the people who sacrificed so much to make us free so you could have your self-worth and pride. Disrespect our flag and national anthem to create hate and God will get you for following Satan.

(God gets the glory!!)

God sent Jesus. Jesus quotes His Father and said, "The Son of man has come to seek and to save which is lost. I am the Way, the Truth, and the Life. No one comes to the Father except through me."

Luke 19:10 (KJV), "For the Son of man is come to seek and to save that which was lost."

John 14:6 (KJV), "Jesus saith unto him, I am the way, the truth, and the life: no man cometh unto the Father, but by me."

This is God's message and a reminder that He sent Jesus and His Son is the One opening the doors to Heaven and we must come through Jesus to get there. I feel sorry for those who do not accept Jesus as God's Son. God made this point very clear. Whether He will give latitude to this is not mentioned. Psalm 19:7 emphasizes God's commandments. The moral laws of God.

# hapter 8

Paul (Saul) Corinthians

PAUL IS AN EVIL MAN WHO IS PERSECUTING CHRISTIANS, THE followers of Jesus, said to the Lord. They were not aware that God knew Paul had the ability to accomplish God's work. Paul had sinned tremendously and was defiant of Jesus. Paul repented, as we can, and he was cleansed. Paul became a great disciple and servant to the Lord and wrote much of the bible.

Many of you do not want to hear these words. It would be jeopardizing your sinful pleasures of sex, lust, greed, or selfish interests. We know that the pleasures of sin are too comfortable for many of you. The satisfaction of your pleasures is too much to give up. The joy you receive from those ways is blended from God's rules and laws.

Your celebrity statis today and the continuation of those ways will eventually wain. You will someday find that does not stabilize your life. The painful results of that lifestyle will gradually become obvious to you! It may take years or a long time before it hits you but believe it. It will happen! Some of you will never find the peace and comfort of a carefree life. The people you are involved in your sinful ways will wear on you. Jealousy from you or them may creep in. One of you will offend the other or tire of their association unless love is part of the occasion. Love is the one thing that holds people together.

I feel sorry for those who do not find love. There may be fondness, but not true love. There may be a feeling of obligation, but not love. Love is so strong; it is not hard to recognize. You will know! Remember: God's love is true love. My takeaway from scriptures is that Love bonded in God is the deepest, strongest, yielding compassions that has ever been unchanging.

Infatuation is in contrast to true love! Some of us will never know what true love is! That is a sad thing, and I am so terribly sorry for them.

Worshipping material things is idol worshipping and a deterrent to realizing that love is more valuable than worldly possessions. To those who are given wealth, much is expecting. Sharing and charity is expected. Luke 12:48 (KJV) The name of our charity family foundation is 12:48.

We will continue to support these comments, even though you may not want to hear them. Someday, it will hit you and you will be transformed! We pray for you to see the perpetual light of God shining on you and in your eyes. That pleasure you have had is superficial. Having no supporting factor for a base or foundation for the future.

When spiritual guidance takes over one's life, it becomes a foundation to build your life on. Oh, the evil one will still try to undermine your faith with temptations and use our weaknesses against us, and we may falter at times, but the spirit still stays in your heart.

God does not lose His faith in our possibilities, and He smiles when we recover from our lust or greed and return to Him for forgiveness of our weaknesses and we are grateful for His love. True happiness only comes when we give God credit for giving us that happiness. God is in charge and He can control all things that affect us. Please get this straight: good, pain, comfort, peace, and tranquility are all in God's hands. He gives and He takes away. Some sinful people have many material things and have power. God may allow that, but He will punish them or rebuke them later, but it is His plan when and where, and the purpose of it all.

(I feel sorry for God) Israelites, the chosen people disobeyed God. He warned them over and over. They didn't listen! God put them in bondage (slavery) twice. Forty years in Egypt by the Assyrians and again in Mesopotamia by the Babylonians.

Today we see disrespect for President Trump. Bible says to respect and honor your ruler or leader. The president is condemned by evil by those who criticized him. God expects obedience to the position. The leader may have faults, but if he is effective and doing God's will, then the accusers are working with the evil that is promoted by Satan. If the leader does evil things, then pray to God for help and vote him or her out. Freedom of choice, God gave us that choice in the U.S. and in our lives.

Acts 9:16 (my take in KJV) – God says, I have chosen Paul.

The U. S. is to be a nation under God and protected from the evil force then tries to take God out of our country. Satan uses evil, and materialistic and power seekers to disrupt God's plans. Reference Exodus 22:18 (KJV) and Ezra 6:10 (KJV).

The temples of the Lord throughout history have been challenged, destroyed, and damaged. Some rebuilt and preserved.

However, the travesty of those times has never disrupted God's love for us!!

God handpicks those who are involved in this process!!

Many of us are able to accomplish great or good things. In business, entertainment, service to others, and be creative to accomplish recognition. Celebrity status, wealth, sports standouts, whatever the degree of success, it is essential to remember and be reminded that God has a hand in it on your behalf.

Let us not be blinded to feel that it is all because of you ... God should be thanked and recognized for getting you there or giving you the opportunity to do it. There are many great and capable people who could have done what you have done, but never got the chance; maybe even better than you? But you were chosen or determined enough to succeed. God still had a hand in it and His grace be honored. God feels good when He is appreciated. I feel sorry for God when He gives gifts and gets no gratitude.

Praise and glory come from the heart, the not head!!

Be humble in your success, do not boast or brag. If you have done something worthy of recognition, let it come from someone else; then it is not bragging, and it is more emphasized in scope, when it comes from someone else and not from you.

To be anointed by our Father in Heaven or by our human biological father is bestowing on us to fulfill their expectations of us. God has a purpose in mind for us. We may think that we are capable of using our talents, energy, and creativity to become accomplished or successful and maybe we can?

Whether we can walk through life and career on our own, and not depend on anyone or anything to get us where we want to go, is the attitude of many. I do not know how many can do that. I do not know that some persons are able to go it alone. I do know that if God did not want you to be accomplished, you would not be!

I do not deny that many people can reach high hurdles because of the talents and physical capabilities they are born with are different for each one of us.

What God expects from us is gratitude and recognition. I feel sorry for God when He gives great talent to someone or someone who is gifted, not realize that there are certain expectations that are expected to show your generosity and willingness to follow God's love and share your good rewards to be helpful to those who are suffering or in need.

This is where your heart becomes your guideline. It is not the gold and material things that can compete with good deeds and gifts that lift up the fallen ... the smile of a wounded child, the bright face of an older person receiving a kind word or a gift or food when they are hungry light up when they encounter someone who cares. Success comes from the heart more than from material items.

A famous person giving their time and attention to others, a child, or adult, can move mountains and create memories for a lifetime. You never know when you do something that you consider inconsequential will come back to you like a revolutionary accomplishment.

God creates these opportunities and lays them in our paths of life. We may notice them and do nothing, or we may know this is a way to see beyond our own personal purposes and into another's needs for assistance. It may seem ever so small in scope and not material at all, but it could be opening a door to the future.

> The path of life when it begins
> The first few days until the end
> The course it takes we do not know
> Not for us, but God to know
> It may be rough, it may be brief
> You do your best and then believe
> It's all laid out along your path
> To pick it up or let it pass
> Thank God you get a second chance.

When you do a good deed or are helpful to someone with kindness and willingly, we may feel a high and gratification that is the Holy Spirit coming to you when you can smile or know that it is going to get better.

When you lose a loved one and your grieving is compelling and seemingly unstoppable, when someone or something makes you realize that it is God's intent and purpose involves that person you love. That is the Holy Spirit telling you that if you trust in God and believe the promises of Christ, you will understand why your loved one is doing God's will, and has been called for a purpose.

God's Holy Spirit is like God's Calvary to be with you at all times and keep God with you on a personal basis. One-on-one with your Father in Heaven. With billions of people, God is one-on-one with you (wow, how can that be?).

God has shown the world who is in Charge. He doesn't feel sorry for those who ignore the fact that only through our Lord, will this country be free of punishment and get back to One Nation Under God!!!! He is offended by many of His people, and by association we will be included in that punishment. I am sorry

He has to go to extremes, but He has been neglected and is such a loving God that we may have pushed Him too far!!!

The coronavirus and extreme weather conditions and wars of different battlegrounds from medical, weaponry, military strength and many soldiers cannot conquer a simple virus. Supernatural weaponry cannot be defeated. We are witnessing Gods power, yet not many of the leaders are asking Him for help.

In Jeremiah, God discusses what worldly pleasures can cause him to be disgusted with us. Seeking worldly pleasures and acting our lives for the flesh or temporary gratifications. The countries of God's people sinning and resisting their Lord can only give God justification and irritation for retaliation.

Punishment is given from God after much patience has worn thin.

Be prepared for retaliation.

Chapter 9

Jeremiah 3:6-25 (KJV)

6 THE LORD SAID ALSO UNTO ME IN THE DAYS OF JOSIAH THE king, Hast thou seen that which backsliding Israel hath done? she is gone up upon every high mountain and under every green tree, and there hath played the harlot. 7 And I said after she had done all these things, Turn thou unto me. But she returned not. And her treacherous sister Judah saw it. 8 And I saw, when for all the causes whereby backsliding Israel committed adultery I had put her away, and given her a bill of divorce; yet her treacherous sister Judah feared not, but went and played the harlot also. 9 And it came to pass through the lightness of her whoredom, that she defiled the land, and committed adultery with stones and with stocks. 10 And yet for all this her treacherous sister Judah hath not turned unto me with her whole heart, but feignedly, saith the Lord. 11 And the Lord said unto me, The backsliding Israel hath justified herself more than treacherous Judah. 12 Go and proclaim these words toward the north, and say, Return, thou backsliding Israel, saith the Lord; and I will not cause mine anger

to fall upon you: for I am merciful, saith the Lord, and I will not keep anger for ever. 13 Only acknowledge thine iniquity, that thou hast transgressed against the Lord thy God, and hast scattered thy ways to the strangers under every green tree, and ye have not obeyed my voice, saith the Lord. 14 Turn, O backsliding children, saith the Lord; for I am married unto you: and I will take you one of a city, and two of a family, and I will bring you to Zion: 15 And I will give you pastors according to mine heart, which shall feed you with knowledge and understanding. 16 And it shall come to pass, when ye be multiplied and increased in the land, in those days, saith the Lord, they shall say no more. My KJV take is the ark of the covenant of the Lord: neither shall it come to mind: neither shall they remember it; neither shall they visit it; neither shall that be done any more. 17 At that time they shall call Jerusalem the throne of the Lord; and all the nations shall be gathered unto it, to the name of the Lord, to Jerusalem: neither shall they walk any more after the imagination of their evil heart. 18 In those days the house of Judah shall walk with the house of Israel, and they shall come together out of the land of the north to the land that I have given for an inheritance unto your fathers. 19 But I said, How shall I put thee among the children, and give thee a pleasant land, a goodly heritage of the hosts of nations? and I said, Thou shalt call me, My father; and shalt not turn away from me. 20 Surely as a wife treacherously departeth from her husband, so have ye dealt treacherously with me, O house of Israel, saith the Lord. 21 A voice was heard upon the high places, weeping and supplications of the children of Israel: for they have perverted their way, and they have forgotten the Lord their God. 22 Return, ye backsliding children, and I will heal your backslidings. Behold, we come unto thee; for thou art the Lord our God. 23 Truly in vain is salvation hoped for from the hills, and from the multitude of mountains: truly in the Lord our God is the salvation of Israel. 24 For shame hath devoured the labour of our fathers from our youth; their flocks and their herds, their sons and their daughters. 25 We lie down in our shame, and our confusion covereth us: for we have sinned against the Lord our God, we and our fathers, from our youth even unto this day, and have not obeyed the voice of the Lord our God.

When King Josiah was ruling Judah, the Lord said to me, "Did you see what unfaithful Israel did?"

She was like a prostitute with her idols on every hill and under every green tree. I said to myself, Israel will come back to me after she does this evil, but she didn't come back. Israel's wicked sister Judah saw what she did, Judah saw that I divorced unfaithful Israel because of her adultery, but that didn't make Israel's wicked sister, Judah afraid. She also went out and acted like a prostitute! She didn't care that she was acting like a prostitute. So, she made her country unclean and was guilty of adultery because she worshipped idols made of stone and wood. Israel's wicked sister didn't even come back to me with her whole heart, but only pretended, says the Lord.

The Lord said in Jeremiah 3:12 (NASB 1995): "Go and proclaim these words toward the north and say, 'Return, faithless Israel,' declares the Lord; 'I will not look upon you in anger. For I am gracious,' declares the Lord; 'I will not be angry forever.'" This shows the mercy given to us and the love and forgiveness the Lord offers.

I will not be angry with you forever. This is so amazing that the Lord goes to such great lengths to allow us to repent. Human behavior would not be that forgiving. Humans would probably say, "enough is enough." They would more than likely be unforgiving after being rejected so many times.

All you have to do is admit your sins, "That you turned against the Lord your God and worshipped gods under every green tree and didn't obey me," says the Lord.

"Come back to me, you unfaithful children," says the Lord. Because I am your master!

God is in charge and can punish us as much as He wants! God is love, and loving God is easy. Satan offers temporary pleasure! God offers internal peace and happiness.

Today if you think about the coronavirus and how God shut the world down, and how "One Nation, Under God" (the USA) should stand united with God. This nation is the only nation built on Judeo-Christian values, and has fallen so far from "In God We Trust," has resembled wicked Israel, we should know that God is aware and He offers forgiveness if we change and acknowledge our sins. He will forgive us!!! If we do not understand and realize the virus is a warning from God, and put Him at the top of our recovery, and ask for His help, then He will send a storm that will encompass the entire United States.

What do you expect from life? Many of us seem to know when we're young what we want to be and keep that desire to completion. Many of us will be placed into a position by circumstances (or God) where our destiny is decided by a person or the place we're in. Many marriages happen because two people are exposed to one another in their environment. Whoever they're dating at the time they think they should marry. Love is powerful! Make sure you know what love is, and not yield to desire or pleasure because love must be forever and not a few hours of pleasure.

Some people just want to get by as easy as they can. If they can exist and avoid working, they will. Others want to leave a legacy or a reputation that is impressive.

How we're influenced can come from many ways. Our parents have a lot of influence on us normally. That influence can be negative or positive. We may think we want to do better than our parents and make them proud of us. Some want to be just like their parents. If their parents are happy with living on welfare, then they might be willing to do the same with their lives. Others want the pride of accomplishment. Some try to improve themselves and end up defeated and give up because they just can't get the break in life that they long for! And expect, thinking they're entitled to it. You have to work hard to succeed, and you have to work hard at your relationships.

Some may get knocked down in life time and time again, but they keep getting up and try again.

Some find a little success and start spending lavishly and get overspent and they forget to save and have financial opportunities available to them. Not planning for the future or having reserves put aside if they run into a crisis.

Creativity is also a part of planning for life. Always be aware when you see or think of a way to make your position in life better. Or find a way to make someone else improve or do better. Giving you a sense of helping someone in need. Spiritual or materially. More rewarding to give than receive!!

Drinking too much or gambling can be a curse! Sins like that can stop success in your life, and make success disappear. They are diseases that are tough to break, and the desire and habit is overwhelming.

Some of the most respected in life are those who fought these demons and beat them. Never criticize a person addicted to drugs, alcohol, or liquor, but try to help them. Few ever recover, but many can with the opportunity for help. The best way to structure a life is to influence it while the person is young. If they don't get the influence from home, then their teachers or coaches can take that responsibility.

Lord, as you look down and see what's in our hearts, know our love for you and for each other. Please bless us and fill us with your knowledge and send us forth to spread your Word. Let us shine with your Holy Spirit and bring others to your Kingdom. For it is Your Love that exalts us in Your Word.

Chapter 10

THE LORD SAYS:

"If the world would find peace, and without conflict the world and countries could start over and would begin to refurbish themselves." Global warming solved, the return of the lost species of animals, plants, vegetation, and return to how God created it! Think about it.

No wars, not one religion seeking to destroy others of different beliefs. No dictators mistreating God's people or the environment. Peace and love for all! No hatred in people.

"Obviously, that will not happen with human nature being what it is." It will take the "destruction" of evil. The evil in human beings and the group of evil makers controlled by Satan. The Tribulation, the Rapture, the millennials, and ultimately Christ's return and rule for a thousand years. That is why the New Earth. "The earth will be refurbished to its original beauty and creatures, crawly things, vegetation and beautiful terrain." There will still be evil or conflicts during the thousand years, but they will be quickly resolved. Satan and evil will cease to exist when God has prevailed. That is when those desires of peace will happen.

If the world today was capable of overriding hate and prejudice, and we all could love each other all over the world, it could happen now. But mankind will not accept through that situation of refusing to love and eliminate hate!

Armageddon, wars, crimes of evil are always the answer until God decides to take charge. Adam and Eve could have prevented all this. If they had gone back to God after being cast out of the Garden and asked for forgiveness, maybe God would have forgiven them? God intended his creation to enjoy the fruits of Eden and love a carefree life and fill His Heaven with followers who would obey Him. God created the Heavens to be filled with His children! His creation has given Him unpleasant developments in His people; plus Satan continually working against Him.

Until the world succumbs to God's commands, we are lost except by following God's laws. He destroyed His human creation once, and now He will pick His true followers and present them to His Kingdom, Paradise! Much like the Garden of Eden.

There is "no other" way to accomplish the problems of evil, hate, lust, power, domination. Preparation for the end is right there in front of you. Talk to your Lord, tend yourself to commitment to God's laws and realize God is Love! You can love! Yield to the will of your Heavenly Father and talk to Him and be children of obedience and do it with "free will" which He so graciously gave you!

God is good! All the time! All the time! God is good!

Genesis 6:5-6-7 (KJV): "5 And God saw that the wickedness of man was great in the earth, and that every imagination of the thoughts of his heart was only evil continually. 6 And it repented the Lord that he had made man on the earth, and it grieved him at his heart. 7 And the Lord said, I will destroy man whom I have created from the face of the earth; both man, and beast, and the creeping thing, and the fowls of the air; for it repenteth me that I have made them."

Destroy His human creation and start over. I feel sorry for God that He had to do that, but He just did not like what His creation had turned into. (And today???)

Suppose you as a human built a mansion and you wanted to invite people who had developed themselves into respectable and honorable people to your home. These people would have to be respected and honest persons. The Lord feels the same way. He invites those who are spiritual and worthy.

hapter 11

Parallel

GOD FACING THE DISPOSAL OF LUCIFER AND HIS FOLLOWERS WAS
about to create Heavens and Earth. Upon creating Earth and
Heavens, He wanted to fill His Heavens with mankind who would
follow His rules and commit their allegiance and worship Him.
He also didn't want people who were just robots, but those - given
free will - would have the chance to decide if they really loved God
as God loved them.

He started with Adam in the Garden of Eden, giving Adam
paradise to live in. No work, stress, fear, or concern of any kind.
Isolated Adam became lonely, so God took a rib from Adam and
gave him Eve.

God's purpose of making was to fill His Heavens. Adam and
Eve failed. Heavens' doors were closed. Poor God made it perfect
and they blew it!!

God didn't intend for life to be so complicated, but with free
will and the evil forces of Satan, it has become a mess. I feel sorry
that we've done this to God and caused Him problems.

God's intentions in His creation was to fill His Heaven. His intentions all the way to the end of time and after Jesus rules the New Earth for a thousand years doesn't change! God's doors are open for redemption all the way to the end of Jesus' rule in the millennium. So God's Will to fill His Heavens is parallel from beginning to the end.

God's love is ever ending to His people until the end of time.

There is a parallel from God's creation from beginning to the end. God's prospective in how He begins our creation to the end of it! The instances between are influenced by the behavior of His creations' actions and behavior. Influenced by evil and emotions, influenced by circumstances that affect individual reactions. God's subjects are not all inclined to follow His Word. Lust, greed, power, all contribute to His people's behavior. The gift of free will is divisive and challenging to everyday reasoning. Procrastinating, excuses, and making a reason to disobey!

In the beginning from Adam and Eve, life came from a living in Paradise to total disruption of the human race.

God has witnessed the process of His creation changes and behavior, and He has addressed them separately, but God has not changed His mind about filling His Kingdom, so the parallel is that many things and people change, but God's purpose for mankind has not changed.

The parallel is that it has been different than expected, but the intent and purpose have not!!

God has watched and controlled the purpose and acted accordingly. He is always in control and always will be, but He gives some leeway to us and thank Heavens, He is a "Loving God". He will forgive and offer us the opportunity to be forgiven, over and over. His patience is unbelievable.

The parallel is that His purpose for mankind is to have all of us in His Kingdom!

In the end, God will do away with evil, Satan, and others. He will also do away with those of us who are evil. Therefore, it is our opportunity not to worship power, material things, and greedy and self-centered actions.

After original sin, God was watching what transpired. He was not pleased. His plan was changing. He watched in despair as His people cast Him aside. Adam and Eve did not pass the information to their descendants who God was, and that He created them. Their behavior was appalling to God. God destroyed them and hoped the next generations would follow His rules. Not so! Noah himself disappointed God.

God's intent is still the same! (Parallel) but happening differently than desired.

Letting free will continue was understood and unchanged God does not want robots. He wants those of us to earn His love by our way of life and being obedient and appreciative of what we have, no matter how meager or plentiful.

After God destroyed the early existence of mankind leaving Noah, Japheth, Ham, Seth, and their wives to start creation of God's children and to fill the earth, God hoped that obedience to His Word would be the mission. The actual results were not as much as God had hoped for. God was not discouraged, but His realization that temptation and the procrastination continued to cause many to seek pleasure over God's promises. Again, God redirected His intent and sought out the ones who were devoted to Him and even redeemed some sinning individuals and encouraged them to change their ways and perform the missions God wanted to accomplish! I think this is witnessed even today!

Examples of people who are given visions of what God wants and picks the individuals who can do what "He wills." They may be sinners or not totally devout, but they change when God's Holy Spirit takes them over.

Lord, oh my Lord, it is so easy to see
Not understand why you sanctify me.
Lord, oh my Lord, it's so easy to fall
Why can't we see how You suffered for all?
Lord, oh my Lord we hope You know that we care
Your blessings to all, just to know that You're there.

I have always been a man of faith. I have always been a man tested by lust and greed, fed by the circumstances of my childhood. Over 25 years ago the Holy Spirit came upon me and allowed me to see the truth of God's and His Son's promises.

I consider myself as one of God's chosen disciples. My life is now consumed in God's Word. I have become a student of the bible and willingly and anxious to talk about the glory waiting for those who are willing to put their trust in Jesus and His (and our) Father.

The visions and dreams that supply God's plans and expectations for me are what inspires me to write and preach for others to understand who God really is. He has a plan for His people (you and I) to follow His Son's teachings and instructions to be with Him in Heaven. It is so visible when you open your eyes.

I believe Heaven will be similar to the Garden of Eden. Abundance of happiness without evil (the Garden of Eden had the presence of Satan), "the difference," and so beautiful and pleasant music will be so soothing and enjoyable. Abundance of all and everything to provide content and comfort.

God created us in His Image, with emotions, some of which are His emotions also.

If that is the case, why wouldn't He also create a Heaven with, as I described, and maybe the Garden of Eden would have some of the same characteristics?

God's Will Be Done!

God's will, human will, free will.

God's intent in the beginning with Adam and Eve was to have His creation to have the ability to choose their behavior. To do right or wrong. Choose how they would live their lives. He knew that would cause Him to lose control over mankind directly, but He also knew that those who loved Him and followed Him would prove their deserving to live in His Kingdom (Paradise).

God is a sensitive, loving God.

My mission in my ministry is to understand God as an individual. What causes Him discomfort or disappointment? God giving us leeway to make our own decisions has not been a total success, when He wants to fill His Heavens, and for those enjoying the rewards and pleasures of Heaven when they follow God's Word. God is not pleased by what He has seen transpire from the beginning of His creation. In Genesis 6:5, God was fed up with His people! His heart was filled with pain! So He destroyed mankind except for Noah and his family. After that as Noah and his family progressed into rebuilding mankind, even Noah disappointed Him.

God is not pleased with the world and its people today!

We are very specific in our spiritual life to pray worship, and praise God. We thank God for what He does and has done for us. We ask Him for many things. We ask him for favors, healing, helping others, and thank God for our blessings. He is our creator, our Heavenly Father, we are His children. We look to Him for guidance and wisdom. We have many requests!! He loves to hear from us. "We love having Him there for us!!"

However: do we ever think about His feelings? How is His day (if that is how Heaven phrases time)? What are God's worries today? How discouraged is He by what is going on in His creation?

God is in control and can do whatever He wants to correct what He thinks is wrong! Just like what will happen to end all the existences of mankind. As we stated previously, there is a parallel to God's creation from beginning to the end. The circumstances of what has transpired and will transpire in between is somewhat irrational and irresponsible. Sinful and cruel, mixed in with loyal followers of God's will!

"God's will be done." In His time.

The scriptures lay out what lies ahead and the destruction that will follow with mankind and earthly. The Rapture, the Tribulation, the Millennium. The New Earth will restore to God's original creation.

This is the ending of the Parallel. That is why the Lord's creation is a parallel. Beginning and end with harmony. In between, confusion, disruption, and the constant conflict among nations and tribes. Greed, lust, grief, suffering, agony, anger, laughter, love, hate, joy, jealousy, compassion. God shares emotions with us. Oh, He does not lust or have greed, but He can witness all the others! This should make us fear and commit to be true followers of the Lord and praise Him constantly!

This is why we need to know God, Himself better.

Think about God's side of things. What is He facing today? Is His day, troubled, or feeling ignored? God is a jealous God, but a loving, forgiving, generous God. He does have His angels, others in His Kingdom, but it is those living in His world that He needs to communicate with. God will pick a person He knows can communicate for Him, or do a job He wants done, and He will use that person to do His will. That person or persons may not be the most devoted or pious person, but God knows He has someone who can do His will!

In understanding God Himself, we must realize and commit to Him. Will never know why God does what He does. It is done in His time!! He decides when and if He will do it! We know that God loves us. That He gives us chance after chance to change our ways. Even to the end of time, after the Rapture, the tribulation and even to the Millennium, the chance to redeem oneself still exists.

God's purpose to create the Heavens and earth was to fill the Heavens with followers that obey Him. This was after God and Lucifer had their disagreement and God cast Lucifer and his followers out of Heaven because they were undermining God's will and rules. Lucifer and his followers formed their own dwelling place and have fought and tried to disrupt God's people and God's plans. Still today and ever since, Satan has been present to get us away from God. Some of their work is boosted by lust, greed, ambition, power, hunger, and pleasurable sin.

God sees this and watches as it pains God to see His people being tempted and falling into the weakness of the human body pleasure and fantasy overrule God's plans for us. Consider the pain it causes God to watch this. "I feel sorry for God."

God is totally aware of what we do and what we think. We are blessed to know that no matter how low we go in our sins that God will forgive us if we repent. Could we be that forgiving?? Could we let our child go through torture, death, and humiliation as an "act of love"? That is what we need to know about God.

If we, as humans, witnessed from the rejection of us from other people by ignoring us and deliberately did things that upset or hurt us, could we be as forgiving and continue to love those who treated or ignored us as we sometimes do to God? Racism, discrimination, bias behavior, can be overcome by forgiveness, and complying with society.

The people I have known and interacted with through the years, very few would be kind and loving enough to forgive and forget and open their arms to welcome you with forgiveness.

It is always a good thing to consider what God goes through with us. Let us put ourselves through that analysis of comparing how we behave when we are faced with those who lie to us, cheat us, rob us, deceive us, destroy our reputation, accuse us falsely, mistreat our children or relatives, misrepresent what we do and treat us unjustly. Could we just let it go and forgive them??? If someone harms you or takes credit for your good deeds. Think about it. Those misdeeds toward you would be painful!! Could you let it go and go back to your life without reacting? God sometimes reacts with punishment, but He still gives them a chance to be forgiven. Can you? Be honest with yourself; it will be hard for you to accept your offenders back into your life.

I feel sorry for God.

We worship Him. God, our creator, our hope for the future. Our Heavenly Father, the creator of all things. He is our salvation. Our place in His decision. Our comforter, our guidance, and our possibility of a place in Paradise, Heaven. We appeal to Him through prayer for our needs, our wishes, our strength, and our problems. We praise Him for His blessings, no matter how small. When we are troubled, in doubt, confusion in us, and understanding of what is happening, He gives us strength, courage, wisdom, comfort, and understanding. Our redeemer, his Son Jesus has given us the open door to His Kingdom. We are all blessed and have a one-on-one relationship with our Lord, but!

"I feel sorry for God."

God is! Was! And always will be the Almighty!

Before God's creation of Heaven and earth, His Kingdom consisted of angels, and His surroundings we do not know. It was paradise we believe and always will be. Comfort and bliss would be my assumption. He had rules and expectations I am sure (our earthly fathers do as well). Lucifer and other angels were rebelling against God's rules. The disagreement came to the conclusion that God cast them out of His Kingdom.

Lucifer and his followers started their own evil domain and have tried to undermine God in all ways. Trying to turn everyone, and everyone that God would create after their falling, out of God's favor.

God was disappointed by Lucifer and his followers. After God had given them what they needed to exist in comfort and tranquility. And they continue to try to disrupt the plans of our Father.

When God decided to create the Heavens and earth, He had a plan. I think He wanted a family. He wanted His people to follow His rules and fill His Heavens with people whose choice was to obey God's rules. God gave "Free will" to all, so they had the choice to be followers of His Word.

Disappointments would follow. I feel bad for God and all who disobey Him. Because it is a loss for all of them.

God intended for His creation to be pleasant, fulfilling life for all to enjoy. However, as a good Father, He wanted all creations to follow His simple guidelines. Free will, and emotions in humans, some emotions God Himself has, cause us to be weak and procrastinate ourselves into sinful ways. Lust, greed, power, material wealth, and physical pleasure interfere without respect and obligations to our Father (humans witness some of these refusals to listen to their earth parents) your children do not always do what you want for them.

God's first people started with one Adam.

When His creation started, He created Heaven and earth and galaxies, cosmos, and universes. Earth is in one universe, but there are many more. He may be still creating more? He does care deeply about His humans here on our planet. Let us not forget that He does continue to watch us closely. He has tried to let us turn all of our troubles over to Him, but free will leads us away from Him, our forgiving creator who gives us chance after chance to mend our ways and some of us ignore His generosity. God tries so hard to lead us to His Kingdom! Sacrificing His Son to open the doors to Heaven after Adam and Eve's betrayal in Eden. Some of us still do not get it!

"I feel sorry for God." He cannot be pleased with us!

Before when Adam was created, God formed the earth, then added water, then vegetation, trees, flowers, bushes to serve in food supply and other activities, then the animals and creatures, including crawly creature. He was pleased with the beauty and watching His creation. Then God created our beginning. Adam was placed in the garden with beautiful lakes and rivers, berries, fruit, and necessities to have a pleasant environment of comfort. Light came from sun and moon.

Adam complained about being lonely, so God generously gave Adam Eve. He put Adam to sleep, took a rib (you know that story). Adam and Eve were happy, what else could they want? They could start to grow the human race! No worries, no work, no rent, no taxes. Paradise! Naked and comfortable, all good!

They had thousands of food sources. God only asked one

simple little thing! Only one! Here comes Satan. "Eve, why don't you eat or taste that fruit. The one God told you not too ..."

"I feel sorry for God." Giving much, asking little ...

Luke 12:48 says it in the KJV bible, to be given much, much is expected.

One tree out of thousands ... 18:48 (KJV). My takeaway from scripture modified.

God watched the disobedience and appeared to them again after the betrayal. They had learned right and wrong. Learned to avoid nakedness and covered themselves with leaves. Disappointed, God sent them out of Heaven. They did not ask for forgiveness, they left to fend for themselves. They had children but did not tell them the mistakes they had made. Total disobedience became the way of life, away from God.

 hapter 12

MY TAKEAWAY FROM READING THE SCRIPTURE GENESIS 6:5 TELLS us of God's disgust. He destroyed all people except Noah's, Japheth's, Seth's, and Ham's spouses, and saved them to start mankind over. God's caring gave us another chance. That chance has not worked again, as far as what God was hoping, and expecting. "I feel sorry for God."

Do not ever underestimate the presence of God in your daily lives. He is always there, always watching. Doing things you do not even realize what He is affecting in your life!!

I am totally dumbfounded by God's love for us and His willing to continue to forgive us for sins and avoiding Him. Billions of us on earth and we have a one-on-one relationship with Him. He knows our heart and our minds. He knows our transgressions and weaknesses. He knows Satan and his followers are working against us and trying to undermine God's will. God knows that when He gave us free will that our procrastination, personal desires, and temptations can persuade us to break the covenants and cause us to stumble. He knows that but continues to love us. Chance after chance to redemption. It is so overwhelming to me to see the Lord so aware and available to us and caring and generous to us. Are we that caring?

The Holy Spirit is God's servant and is working with us. The Spirit is with us. His presence keeps God informed. Everything we do is recorded. God is, was, and always with us. I cannot imagine the total love He extends to us. I get chills when I think about desire for us to be able to enter His Kingdom by our good news from Jesus, the goodness of God: all the time!! As sinners who repent can live in paradise through His glory, I find it hard to believe that God is so loving and forgiving and, we disappoint Him so often.

I have often heard people say, "God knows my heart, I don't need to pray." I have heard people say, "I go to church at [church] because its service is only 45 minutes." Are they going to spend time with God or just feel they are fulfilling an obligation? If you are not willing to spend an hour or more with your worshipping your God after all He has done for us, then why should God expect that you are sincere? I have known people who claim to be spiritual, that their devotion is only skin deep, a veneer to make people believe that you are a true Christian willing to do God's work of helping others, being disciples of God's Word. The bible is full of good stories and parables that make you think! Learning about God's Word and how He works with His servants is interesting, educational, and heartwarming. It shows you just how great God is!

hapter 13

IN THE OLD TESTAMENT, GOD SOUNDS LIKE HIS ACTIONS ARE different while dealing more directly with those who have original sin, the pagans. However, some of the most important lessons and events with God's followers' performances, they are so interesting!! God's emotions are more prevalent in hearing those stories. From Noah, Abraham, Moses, Isaac, Jacob, Isaiah, and others. Those stories also give us insight into God's personal feelings. Deborah was a woman who proved women can do God's work as well as men.

As God watches us then and now, there is evidence that He observes and sees His creation every day and knows what our intimate being is performing in our actions.

How does God have day-to-day contact with us when there are billions of us? It is the Holy Spirit, God's calvary, that keeps doing His assessment of our doing.

[Father, Lord, we love and appreciate You! And what you have done for us. Let us open our hearts to Your will and be worthy of Your Son's promises! We know we are blessed. We are so grateful and fortunate to have Your love. Go with us as we share Your love and spread Your Word and good will. For it is through Your kindness that we learn by example. Praise You, Lord, and Jesus.]

We have a Creator who only wants the best for us. A God that never intended for it to be so difficult to live in a sinful world and be deserving to be able to be delivered into His Kingdom. As we mentioned in the parallel of God's creation, He wanted to fill His Heavens with all of us. The status of the behavior of today's people is different today. Starting from the beginning, it would have been a pleasant journey to the door of Heaven. Sin and destructive behavior had created, with the help of Satan, a different and more difficult life to live and follow God's rules and exist in Godly ways of spiritual living. Peer pressure, greed, lust, and all the temptations and social scrutiny.

It is incriminating at times and in different social or working instances to swear your allegiance to God (your Father). Jesus said, if you do not recognize me, I will not recognize you to my Father. My takeaway from reading the scripture.

You will find that as you claim your allegiance to God and Jesus, you will encounter different responses for those who are present. Some will say nothing, some will reject you, or some will acknowledge their own faith. I find very few will openly reject the subject of our Lord. I feel some people are just waiting for someone to approach them. The have faith on their minds, they just do not know how to approach it and when someone brings it up, they are anxious to talk about it. I was leaving our community one late afternoon and stopped my car to say hi to two neighborhood ladies that were friends of ours. I congratulated them on their exercise. One of them said, "Where are you headed?" I said. "I'm on my way to bible study." "Oh, what church do you go to?" I told them and asked if they and their husbands would want to go to church with us some Sunday. They both said yes. There have been many times I have mentioned my faith at social events and got interest from some to attend church with us. We always pray over our food for blessings when eating at home, but also with others when we eat with others, close friends or not. No one ever complains and sometimes when we are out, they ask if I am going to say grace or ask me to "say grace."

When dining out with family or friends, we always say grace and the people around us, I can see them, show us respect by being quiet. Sometimes strangers will stop at our table on their way out and comment on seeing us say grace and they are positive in their remarks.

The Lord's disappointment with Adam and Eve in the Garden of Eden and sent them out, caused God the stress of knowing. His intent to fill the earth with God's followers was stopped. When Adam and Eve left and did not have contact with God, they did not talk to their descendants about God and Heaven. They did not pass the greatness and grace of their Creator. Their descendants had little knowledge of who God really was! Therefore, the earth became full of evil since the knowledge of what God could do for them. Personal pleasure and selfish existence were the way of life. Ruthless and evil prevailed! As we knew before from Genesis 6:5-6-7, it tells us that God lost His patience and hope for saving those on earth! That is my takeaway from reading the scripture.

Noah was living his life as God wished all would do. God chose Noah to save mankind of his family and start the human race over again. God mentions His sadness for having to do that to His people, and "I feel sorry for God" for having to do that because I know God was hurting for being pushed that far!

When you think about what Adam and Eve caused, and then

developed a Godless world, there were few opportunities for converting people to God's spirituality. God could see no future for things to change.

Understanding God is a pursuit that has fascinated me, because He has done and continued to do so much for us, and we just do not think about how ignored He is, except for the praises and thanks that we give Him, and the prayers where we ask for and request what we need in our lives or prayers for others who are in needy situations.

We do not know if God is overridden with failures of our human weaknesses and the undermining of Satan and his demons and followers against God's plans. We, as humans, can have stress and disappointments from our children, or families, and relations. We can be having a depressing day or upset over a negative act, and someone comes to you to tell you about their troubles or ask you to do something for them, that you really are not wanting to do that. But, as a good Christian or compassionate person, listen and counsel, or perform their request, even though you are hurting inside.

I think God has those similar situations, actually we know He does, so we need to realize that and wish God a good day and a reversal of those who reject Him. For such a loving God and the One who wants the best for us, and gives us chance after chance to reform and prepare ourselves for salvation time after time, but often keeps getting rejected by His creation. Think about what God goes through and has for thousands of years! It is not difficult, what He expects, not always easy either, but it is well worth it when you realize you may be satisfying a temporary desire for a short time, but losing eternal happiness in paradise. I feel sorry for God to see what He is trying to lead us to, and we just think about the pleasure of the moment. Our emotions have to be under control in the right way, and that is to have God and His Spirit in our minds and our hearts, and our brain.

Many people are reluctant to answer His call. They can be ashamed to let others hear them pray or proclaim God's Word for fear of rejection by their friends or relatives. Being open in your faith is challenging for some. They do not want to be preached to because if they hear about the Almighty, it may make them feel guilty. Yes! It may make them realize their sins come to mind and they do not want to be reminded that the pleasure they seek are against God's wishes. Deep down they believe in God and Heaven, but they do not want to hear about it. They will even reject friends in order to not hear the recognition or reference to God in prayer or discussions. Their guilt is not wanting to discuss their sinful behavior. If you get them in private, they sometimes will profess their faith, but that does not mean they will change their actions or behavior.

Look at Peter, the disciple, the rock. Lead follower of Christ. Refuses in public to acknowledge Jesus. His personal safely was at stake! Maybe it is more complex than that. If Peter had been captured or put to death, the leader of Jesus' team would be gone. Lots of possibilities exist. There is no reason for us to disown our Maker today!

God's chosen people, the Israelites, have been another reason for feeling sorry for God. Before the coming of Jesus, the Israelites were one of God's main focuses. They were sinful and rejecting of God. God watched them worshiping other god-like subjects and ignoring His Word. He sent them warning after warning. No change! He put them in bondage for 40 years in Egypt. After 40 years, God decided to free them. Moses led them out. They didn't go back to God, but became sinful again. God will not give up on trying to convince us to repent. His patience is amazing!

Only two countries in the world have their beginning from God. Israel, God's chosen, and the United States, founded under the principles of "created under God." Judeo-Christian principles are the basis to keep "one nation under God."

Unfortunately, Israel and the United States have both caused God many regrets by their ignoring of God's Will. God has protected both of these nations though the years, and do they appreciate that? Many of us in society do thank God, but our government and leaders think they can keep us safe and functioning spiritually as human leaders, and brag about how they are going to do things to make us better; but they leave God out of the equation ... wrong! Without God's help, we are missing who is in charge.

Praise the Lord for being with us every day. You have paved our lives to the present! We stumbled for years in our sins and inequities, and You have brought us to our passion of knowing Your love and we have seen the light of Your foundation.

We have tasted the fruit of Your vines of Love and graced us with Your mercy. Praise You for lifting us out of darkness to the light that burns for our salvation and shows the path to righteousness as we open our hearts and swear our devotion!

Please let Your Holy Spirit continue to be with us!

As we know, the Spirit is our true connection to You!

 hapter 14

WE KNOW THE POWER OF REDEMPTION AND WE KNOW YOUR power correction. In Numbers 12, my summary is we learn of God's displeasure of us when we speak against God's servants. Mariam and Aaron spoke about and against Moses.

Numbers 12: "And Miriam and Aaron spake against Moses because of the Ethiopian woman whom he had married: for he had married an Ethiopian woman. 2 And they said, Hath the Lord indeed spoken only by Moses? hath he not spoken also by us? And the Lord heard it. 3 (Now the man Moses was very meek, above all the men which were upon the face of the earth.) 4 And the Lord spake suddenly unto Moses, and unto Aaron, and unto Miriam, Come out ye three unto the tabernacle of the congregation. And they three came out. 5 And the Lord came down in the pillar of the cloud, and stood in the door of the tabernacle, and called Aaron and Miriam: and they both came forth. 6 And he said, Hear now my words: If there be a prophet among you, I the Lord will make myself known unto him in a vision, and will speak unto him in a dream. 7 My servant Moses is not so, who is faithful in all mine house. 8 With him will I speak mouth to mouth, even apparently, and not in dark speeches; and the similitude of the Lord shall he behold: wherefore then were ye not afraid to speak against my servant Moses? 9 And the anger of the Lord was kindled against them; and he departed. 10 And the cloud departed from off the tabernacle; and, behold, Miriam became leprous, white as snow: and Aaron looked upon Miriam, and, behold, she was leprous. 11 And Aaron said unto Moses, Alas, my lord, I beseech thee, lay not the sin upon us, wherein we have done foolishly, and wherein we have sinned. 12 Let her not be as one dead, of whom the flesh is half consumed when he cometh out of his mother's womb. 13 And Moses cried unto the Lord, saying, Heal her now, O God, I beseech thee. 14 And the Lord said unto Moses, If her father had but spit in her face, should she not be ashamed seven days? let her be shut out from the camp seven days, and after that let her be received in again. 15 And Miriam was shut out from the camp seven days: and the people journeyed not till Miriam was brought in again. 16 And afterward the people removed from Hazeroth, and pitched in the wilderness of Paran." My summary is that Miriam served seven days of penance.

Chapter 15

Apostles

GOD'S HOLY SPIRIT IS MORE AMAZING AND MORE ACCOMPLISHED than we might imagine. The activity of the Spirit, how it works, and what it accomplishes is far greater and encompassing than what we might realize. As with God, one will have difficulty in what they are involved in our lives. Again we understand what the Holy Spirit is and who God is, but do we try to get a full understanding of how intimate they are in our lives!

We need to dwell in what God's emotions are; we know His plans for us, do we know how many times He has to alter His plans? His observations of our human existence and how we do things that make God review His expectations and adjust to our weaknesses.

The reason we can have a one-on-one relationship with God since there are billions of us, is because of the Holy Spirit! As when Jesus left the Last Supper, He told the apostles to remain where they were finishing their dinner, and His Father would give them a gift. The gift of the Holy Spirit.

The apostles were to go out and spread the Good News of Jesus, opening the door to Heaven and convert the people to Christianity. There was no backup to their mission, no support system, except God. If they failed, the mission would be lost! But because of the Holy Spirit with them, God knew they would succeed. To that point, let us talk about how the Holy Spirit is the work horse for God ...

Do you really understand the entire scope of the Spirit? Think about it! The Spirit is the one who covers us in our contact with God. Billions of us!

Prayer is lifted to God in many ways. In the name of the Father, and the Son, and the Holy Spirit. Understand the significance of that. Prayer is a communication with God. Simple conversation is fine. Prayer does not have to be in glorified words. Just normal conversation.

Jesus prayed continually. That was His way of keeping in touch with His Father. That is also the way we keep in touch with our Heavenly Father.

As apostles, their job was to relay God's words and the teaching of Jesus. They were teachers. The Holy Spirit was their support system. We are disciples if we speak what we have learned. As a further analysis, we as disciples, also need to be teachers and preachers of the message of God's scriptures.

Matthew 5:1-20 (KJV)

1 And seeing the multitudes, he went up into a mountain: and when he was set, his disciples came unto him: 2 And he opened his mouth, and taught them, saying, 3 Blessed are the poor in spirit: for theirs is the kingdom of heaven.

4 Blessed are they that mourn: for they shall be comforted.

5 Blessed are the meek: for they shall inherit the earth.

6 Blessed are they which do hunger and thirst after righteousness: for they shall be filled.

7 Blessed are the merciful: for they shall obtain mercy.

8 Blessed are the pure in heart: for they shall see God.

9 Blessed are the peacemakers: for they shall be called the children of God.

10 Blessed are they which are persecuted for righteousness' sake: for theirs is the kingdom of heaven.

11 Blessed are ye, when men shall revile you, and persecute you, and shall say all manner of evil against you falsely, for my sake.

12 Rejoice, and be exceeding glad: for great is your reward in heaven: for so persecuted they the prophets which were before you.

13 Ye are the salt of the earth: but if the salt have lost his savour, wherewith shall it be salted? it is thenceforth good for nothing, but to be cast out, and to be trodden under foot of men.

14 Ye are the light of the world. A city that is set on an hill cannot be hid.

15 Neither do men light a candle, and put it under a bushel, but on a candlestick; and it giveth light unto all that are in the house.

16 Let your light so shine before men, that they may see your good works, and glorify your Father which is in heaven.

17 Think not that I am come to destroy the law, or the prophets: I am not come to destroy, but to fulfil.

18 For verily I say unto you, Till heaven and earth pass, one jot or one tittle shall in no wise pass from the law, till all be fulfilled.

19 Whosoever therefore shall break one of these least commandments, and shall teach men so, he shall be called the

least in the kingdom of heaven: but whosoever shall do and teach them, the same shall be called great in the kingdom of heaven.

20 For I say unto you, That except your righteousness shall exceed the righteousness of the scribes and Pharisees, ye shall in no case enter into the kingdom of heaven.

hapter 16

WHEN GOD MADE HIS CHOSEN PEOPLE, THE ISRAELITES, HE HELD them in a special significance. They were a chosen race from Abraham, Jacob, and their descendants. David falls in that lineage. Jesus was a descendant of David. As early as 900-800 B.C. God was discouraged with the Israelites. He gave them warning after warning to stop their sinful ways. God let the Assyrians (the world's first terrorists) attack Israel as a warning and that attack was overpowered. The warning was not enough to cause the Israelites to change. So, in 832 B.C. the ruthless Assyrians conquered Israel and put the Israelites in bondage (slavery) for 40 years in Egypt. You know that story, but it was not what God preferred for them. It was to punish them! "I feel sorry for God" because these were His special people. God had tried very hard to get them to follow His rules, which were not that hard, and they let Him down.

"I am sure you can think of an incident in your life when you have had a similar experience."

God's compassion led Him to rescue His children from bondage and sent Moses to set them free. Moses was not prepared in his own mind to do that, but God explained it to Moses and how He would see that the power of God would guarantee Moses' success. Supernatural assistance. My takeaway of Exodus 7:13 is, "And he hardened Pharaoh's heart, that he hearkened not unto them; as the Lord had said."

God, as always, and even today, picks the person or persons who can get the job done, not necessarily someone who is without sin. There are many examples since God made mankind, which God chooses someone to do His missions who are someone you would least expect Him to choose. There is a distinct possibility that many world leaders are in power because of God's confidence in that person to do God's Will. This goes back to the beginning of time. However, Satan has also put people in power to be evil in their governance. Evil dictators and leaders of some providence can cause torture and death and suffering to innocent persons and families. (This is not God's work. It is evil.) The Holy Spirit was not and will not be with those who are in defiance of God's Holy Word.

During the birth date of Jesus' birth, you need to pay attention to the atmospheric presence of the Holy Spirit. This is God's way of recognizing the sacrifice of His Son (Jesus) given for forgiveness of sin to be punished and tortured as an "act of love." God's gift to open the doors to Heaven. Our greatest Christmas gift ever!!!

"Dwell on that," do not just touch on it! Give it deep thought: what you (you) got that day!!! You got the gift of eternal life! Otherwise, you would be doomed to wander and be lost forever or be consumed by the evil one.

It is easy to generalize God, His Son, and His Spirit. But you should individualize it to you as a person benefitting from God's love for you. If you cannot individualize this, then I feel sorry for you! I feel bad when we don't realize how special we are to our Lord. It is very important that we know the extent of our disappointments we cause God. His own chosen people have caused Him much pain and God has retaliated several times because of His disgust!

This has been disturbing to God for generations and even today (maybe more so).

Our country, the U.S., formed as one nation under God, is close to retaliation because we have turned our backs, many of us, on God. We have had our warnings and ignored them. Our president is sent from God, I believe, because of what he is doing. Recognizing Palestine as the capital of Israel. Getting prayers back on the military and schools, one nation "under God" back in our Pledge of Allegiance, the Ten Commandments displayed, and putting your hand over your heart or saluting during our National Anthem. Many organizations and groups and people would like to get God out of our country. Do "we" do our part in the movement to keep God foremost in the daily expressions of God's presence? Are we disciplined in our actions and expression of God's continual presence in our lives?

We are totally exposed to our Lord. He knows what we are doing every day and hour. We cannot ignore the fact that we are exposed continually and constantly to our Maker! He may not react to us immediately, but in His time, He will have that behavior recorded in His mind.

His presence is there always. He understands free will: He gave it to us. He understands our weaknesses. "He gets it." We are humans! But do not think because God loves us and forgives us when we repent, that it is okay to weaken, at times. That is not good logic. Our time to die is not written in a ledger unless God writes it. Your time could be close. We do not know! "Except that dying is a given."

Interesting that people when they get old, or ill, they turn to God. Hypocritical maybe, but God always welcomes with open arms.

I feel sorry for God for the rejections He gets! I feel sorry for you if you are not getting it.

As we approach the birthday of Jesus each year, think about that birth and what it means to us. That night was beautiful and clear and full of stars that shone brightly in the Heavens. Let us think about our gifts of life that we are sharing. The love of family and friends. That light perpetual continues to shine and light the way to our salvation. The Holy Spirit helps to prepare for that day when in the glory and praise, and raise us to our new beginning in the Kingdom where pain, suffering, fear, stress, and worry will be replaced with a love, peace and with the Holy Spirit, of love, and in the presence of God and His Son, Jesus. "We honor You, Lord, for that gift of peace and happiness for eternity.

How can we not know that this is God's plan for us since the beginning of creation?

Let us be worthy of the promises of Christ. Let our human weaknesses be overcome by common sense of knowing that being in God's graces is there, right in front of you! God watches us and understands our temptations and weakness. Are a few hours of pleasure worth the loss of our opportunity? God is good, all the time! We are all sinners, but we can all be disciples, also. Being a disciple is so uplifting. You can feel the Holy Spirit working with you. Your spirituality is an opportunity to be infectious to others. It makes God smile and I do not have to feel sorry for God.

Prejudice, racism, and bigotry are dividing us and causing

different ethnic groups who use the race card will cause problems as long as they take their defensive stand against one another.

I love my Asian friends! I love my African American friends! I love my Hispanic friends! I love all my friends, and guess what? It is not the color of their skin. It is the love of God in their hearts.

If you want to improve racial conditions, "look in the mirror!" Be the kind of a person that others see the basis of your heart!

I know the injustice that has happened in the past. And I know that some of these injustices still happen. They happen because hatred is in some, not many, but some people in the world. It is Satan working against God's plan for us.

The parallel of God's Creation is that His purpose is as God has pointed out very clearly ... that His intentions from the beginning of time is to fill His Heavens and Kingdom. Scripture and research show that the rapture and tribulations are not the end of His efforts to give us all opportunity after opportunity to convert ourselves to be worthy of His Love. He loves and reigns and has a plan. Several times He calls His deserving children into His Kingdom.

God is well designed because He knows and understands us. As soon as we are totally committed to God's laws, He will call us to Heaven. Maybe not immediately, but when He wants to. The Israelites, His special chosen ones, have been the most difficult since the beginning. Oh, don't get me wrong, the rest of us aren't always quick to get it either.

God continues clear to the end to convert all of us to His paradise. Although it should be very compelling, it's not because Satan and temptation keep some of us complacent and feeling we don't need God in our lives. Again, I feel sorry for them and our Lord.

It's interesting that there will be more than one rapture. They may be called different, but it's still a collection of believers. Then going forward until the millennium ends, there is still the open option of accepting Jesus as His Son and the only door to Heaven. How great is the Trinity of our Maker? God "is" love.

The disruption of God's parallel is continually being attacked by Satan with temptations and events on productions to divert us from following God's purpose and offering pleasure. Sinful actions that give us the satisfaction of a temporary desire. A short time physical attraction or the ability to gain wealth or material possessions.

When we become obsessed with wealth or material collections and make them the things you worship, then they become a false God you're worshipping. Having wealth or wide recognition is not a sin, but is more difficult for wealth and prominent positioned persons to get to Heaven. That depends on how you got it and how you use it. There are many ways to success, but the ones who do it with God in their lives are more successful.

God's parallel intensions from creation to the end of times gives us great insight about human behavior. Free will and temptations and sinful nature can take many of us on a path of self-pride, greed, superior attitude, and selfishness. Even when we're out of line, God still loves us and gives us chances to become kind and generous. God smiles when we put Him in our life and help promote goodness. You may think you're important and proud, but you're really only one of God's creations and you'll answer to Him, just like we do. Your opinion is no more important than a street vendor. Your social position won't last forever. New generations will not remember you, but "God will." Your high and mighty attitude will bring you grief in the future and maybe depression. Be like our Lord and love everybody. No prejudice and love with love in your heart.

The haters will be punished by God!!! Do not let the few cause all society to be affected.

Jackie Robinson broke the barrier for blacks to be in professional baseball by just ignoring the slurs and mistreatment and rejection of him. God picked Jackie because he could take it and rise above it!

Be the type of person who projects love and respect for others. Do not separate yourself with what you wear or how you wear it. Be distinctive in your speech. Instead of calling for non-conformance, give a little and look responsible. I know some will say, "I'm my own person, and I'm going to show my difference." Good luck! Being different can be okay until your kids want to be different, then their kids want to be different, then 150 years later we have bigotry on both sides.

The people in authority need to be taught to be equal and just to all they encounter. That change "has to be made." We must forgive the past injustices of the past, and there were many!! Hard to do, but God and The Spirit will help.

I am a Native American. I know what my mom and grandparents went through. I lived with the people who were prejudice. My relations and ancestors went through terrible abuse! We did not try to be different; we worked through it!! We did not ask for benefits or entitlements. We worked to make ourselves fit in and be a part of society.

It has to start with you. You can change all this resentment and show you are equal and want to fit in and be successful in life. It starts with God's being forgiving, and you also. Try to love your neighbor and quit blaming the past. Let us build a life of acceptance and ignore the idiots who are led by Satan.

When I look at the successful ethnic individuals in the world, and see how they started, and how many come from humble beginnings, it shows us that prejudice and rejection are not there. I have witnessed ethnic people work hard, support their families, and start their own business. It may be in various professions, but they had ambition and mindset for success.

America still offers all of us regardless of faith, color, creed, or any dynamic to have a good life and earn enough to <u>not</u> become slaves of the government. Not to be dependent on others. What pride and accomplishments to stand up to self-sufficiency some people cannot because of personal physical restrictions or sickness or disease, but if physically able to do anything, there are jobs for you.

Chapter 17

Fellowship in God

TRUE CHRISTIAN FELLOWSHIP IS BASED ON CARING AND LOOKING after each other. Our forefathers had it right. Share with neighbors and others. Be generous and observant. The true fellowship is with God and His Son, Jesus. From them comes the development of a loving heart. We learn to love one another! It leads us to act together for the good of all.

Fellowship takes all individuals to open their minds and hearts to not judge others. Try to find the good in persons and not dwell on negatives and overlook some shortcomings and be flexible and understanding.

First impressions are sometimes wrong. What you've heard or how you felt the first time you met them may not be how they are at all. After you get to know them and understand them may give you a different opinion.

Fellowship requires effort and desire.

In different environments when strangers are together, friendships and fellowship are needed. Troops in military service, in hospitals or assignments in different areas. Those together in recovery from injury, disease, addiction, or mental problems need fellowship. In battlefields, it's even more essential.

My summary of Matthew 25:34-46 is that God says: what you do for the least of my people, so you do unto me.

God uses His people to accomplish His missions. They may not be the most devout or pious, or even the best Christians, but He uses the ones that He knows can get the job done.

God knows us all, and we can be one-on-one with Him even though there are billions of people. He watches us and helps us when we deserve it.

Love your neighbor as you love yourself.

Enjoy fellowship from all that you can.

We need a daily thanksgiving to our Father who's love, and forgiveness shows how "hard" God tries to make us worthy of the promises of Christ. I feel sorry for God and anyone who tries to help us and offer us improvement and we turn our backs on them. Our parents are a good example.

Thanksgiving for God

We have a day of thanksgiving every year! The settlers from the beginning were given the way to survive when they landed in America by teaching the pilgrims to grow crops for food and share food with them. The Native Americans were kind to these strangers and the thanks for this kindness extends to today.

We all have much to be thankful for. Do we always realize that we should be grateful for what we have, even though it may not be much? God gives us what we have and uses us for His work.

We should be thankful to live free. Even though our freedom is challenged by Satan and outside sources, our civil rights and love for our freedom compels us to challenge those forces of religious zealots and militants ready to destroy our beliefs. Our government tries to interfere with our lives and rights under the constitution as well.

We don't always appreciate what we get for nothing and don't appreciate what the government gives us or a friend, family member, or parent. We don't take care of what we receive for nothing, as well as we do for something we work hard to pay for.

Satan is active and obstructs God's plans as much as possible and works on us to disregard God's rules and not be thankful.

There are forces that are trying to take God our of our lives. Take prayers our of schools, In God We Trust from our currency. Remove the Ten Commandments from courts and public places, our Pledge of Allegiance without One Nation Under God, prayer in our military, and issues of abortions and marriages.

We should give our thanks and be grateful for all our blessings.

God has given us so much! His Son's suffering (could you have done that to your son?) everything we have, we owe to Him. Our free will leaves it up to us to gain Grace.

Thanksgiving should lead us to generosity. To those in need, to our fellow brothers and sisters and those we witness.

This will make God smile.

Chapter 18

THOSE THAT DON'T FEEL SORRY FOR GOD, WILL FIND OUT THAT they will feel sorry for themselves. In Ezekiel, we read the War of Gog and Magog. My summary of scripture in Ezekiel 38:12 it says the Muslim countries will enlist Russia to join them (the Arabs) to defeat Israel. 3000 years ago Asaph was complaining about the enemies surrounding Israel. Not much change in 3000 years, but now it's getting closer to erupting.

The invading armies will be defeated by supernatural powers of God. Ezekiel 39:4 in the mountains of Israel. Even the Israelites will recognize that the Lord won this battle for them. Many will open their hearts to the Lord. Thousands of Jews will recognize Jesus as the son of God. This essential to entering Heaven.

Today the Lord our God gives us witness to His power. He's always in charge! A tiny virus stops the world economy and stops public events, even churches are closed. Out future depends on God as it always has! If we don't recognize that God can stop the coronavirus, He will send a storm that will cover the entire United States at one time.

We are in or about to be in the Tribulations. Be thinking what you want to do and where you will go. I don't know that the Rapture will be before or after the Tribulations will start. Doesn't matter! God's parallel is still the same. He wants His children with Him, but only if we follow His words and live through Him and His Son.

The Rapture will protect those from the wrath of God but that doesn't prevent the others left behind from being able to repent and have another chance to go to The Kingdom. The anti-Christ will appear and try to rule the world. He will have tough times in gaining control. God is allowing Satan to have his chance, but God will watch over what's happening and let Satan go so far and then stopping him. After Satan and evil's last chance they will be banished in a dark hole and isolated for a thousand years and afterwards reappear only to be destroyed by the fire of God.

I feel sorry for those of us that do not read the scriptures and see the prophesies as they unfold. I feel sorry for God that He has to watch the disobedience that His people when He warns us and encourages us to see that His loving and forgiving and hoping we will see the perpetual light and follow. "He is in charge." "He is here." He is providing and caring and all He asks is commitment. Praise Him, bless Him, and ask Him how His day is going? It's not all about you. It's also about Him. Give Him your devotion for His Glory, His Kingdom, and His Power! Psalm 136 says His love endures forever.

It's interesting that Armageddon will take place in the area where Christians have always had conflict and wars in that area through those years have drawn the USA and other countries into those conflicts.

Maybe it's part of God's overall plan to expose those who defy God's Word. The apostles started out from there to spread God's words and the promises of Jesus Christ. That Holy Land has been a focal point for God's creation. Again I say, look beyond the obvious and dwell on what God is thinking. Our whole existence in this world is tied together and is parallel to God's purpose in creating the universe and the world. If we think beyond our own routine life, there is a purpose for all of us. Praise the Lord.

God didn't make man and the world to be "peaches and cream." He made it complicated. With "free will" and Satan's continual attempt to disrupt God's plans. And ... God allows Satan to interfere because that allows God to see the devout and true believers and followers. He doesn't want those who only claim to be spiritual and committed. God sees us and know our hearts. Not just a veneer of faith over a person who has ulterior thoughts.

When wrong is done to one person from an evil person, God may not respond quickly, but in His own time the misdeed will be accounted for.

106 billion people have walked the earth over the last 50,000 years. Today over 700 billion are on the earth. That number increases every minute.

What is your purpose in life? The main purpose is to prepare for the Kingdom of God. To prepare for you ...???

I like it when God smiles in appreciation for seeing you hearing and complying to His Will.

Starting with 1 Corinthians my summary is that these will make God smile, then there is nothing to be sorry for: God or you!

These are all from the King James Bible.

1 Corinthians 10:31 "Whether therefore ye eat, or drink, or whatsoever ye do, do all to the glory of God."

1 Timothy 4:8 "For bodily exercise profiteth little: but godliness is profitable unto all things, having promise of the life that now is, and of that which is to come."

Proverbs 17:22 "A merry heart doeth good like a medicine: but a broken spirit drieth the bones."

Proverbs 16:24 "Pleasant words are as an honeycomb, sweet to the soul, and health to the bones."

God's Promises of Deliverance

Matthew 6:13 (KJV) "And lead us not into temptation, but deliver us from evil: For thine is the kingdom, and the power, and the glory, for ever. Amen."

Psalm 59:1-2 (KJV) "Deliver me from mine enemies, O my God: defend me from them that rise up against me. Deliver me from the workers of iniquity, and save me from bloody men."

God's Promises of Purpose

Colossians 3:23 (KJV) "And whatsoever ye do, do it heartily, as to the Lord, and not unto men."

Ephesians 2:10 (KJV) "For we are his workmanship, created in Christ Jesus unto good works, which God hath before ordained that we should walk in them."

Ephesians 3:20 (KJV) "Now unto him that is able to do exceeding abundantly above all that we ask or think, according to the power that worketh in us."

Deuteronomy 28:12 (KJV) "The Lord shall open unto thee his good treasure, the heaven to give the rain unto thy land in his season, and to bless all the work of thine hand: and thou shalt lend unto many nations, and thou shalt not borrow."

Psalm 84:11 (KJV) "For the Lord God is a sun and shield: the

Lord will give grace and glory: no good thing will he withhold from them that walk uprightly." Isaiah 50:7 (KJV) "For the Lord God will help me; therefore shall I not be confounded: therefore have I set my face like a flint, and I know that I shall not be ashamed." My summary of the scripture.

Proverbs 28:25 (KJV) "He that is of a proud heart stirreth up strife: but he that putteth his trust in the Lord shall be made fat." My summary of the scripture.

God's Promises of Love

Romans 8:37-39 (KJV) "Nay, in all these things we are more than conquerors through him that loved us. For I am persuaded, that neither death, nor life, nor angels, nor principalities, nor powers, nor things present, nor things to come, Nor height, nor depth, nor any other creature, shall be able to separate us from the love of God, which is in Christ Jesus our Lord."

1 John 4:9-11 (KJV) "In this was manifested the love of God toward us, because that God sent his only begotten Son into the world, that we might live through him. Herein is love, not that we loved God, but that he loved us, and sent his Son to be the propitiation for our sins. Beloved, if God so loved us, we ought also to love one another."

God's Promises of Wisdom

1 Corinthians 1:25 (KJV) "Because the foolishness of God is wiser than men; and the weakness of God is stronger than men."

Colossians 2:2-3 (KJV) "That their hearts might be comforted, being knit together in love, and unto all riches of the full assurance of understanding, to the acknowledgement of the mystery of God, and of the Father, and of Christ; In whom are hid all the treasures of wisdom and knowledge."

Proverbs 15:12 (KJV) "A scorner loveth not one that reproveth him: neither will he go unto the wise."

God's Promises of Friendship

Ecclesiastes 4:9-10 (KJV) "Two are better than one; because they have a good reward for their labor. For if they fall, the one will lift up his fellow: but woe to him that is alone when he falleth; for he hath not another to help him up."

Proverbs 13:20 (KJV) "He that walketh with wise men shall be wise: but a companion of fools shall be destroyed.

God's Promises of Guidance

Isaiah 14:27 (KJV) "For the Lord of hosts hath purposed, and who shall disannul it? and his hand is stretched out, and who shall turn it back?"

God's Promises of Peace

Philippians 4:6-7 (KJV) "Be careful for nothing; but in every thing by prayer and supplication with thanksgiving let your requests be made known unto God. And the peace of God, which passeth all understanding, shall keep your hearts and minds through Christ Jesus."

2 Thessalonians 3:16 (KJV) "Now the Lord of peace himself give you peace always by all means. The Lord be with you all."

Romans 5:1 (KJV) "Therefore being justified by faith, we have peace with God through our Lord Jesus Christ."

God's Promises of Hope

Psalm 25:5 (KJV) "Lead me in thy truth, and teach me: for thou art the God of my salvation; on thee do I wait all the day."

Psalm 25:21 (KJV) "Let integrity and uprightness preserve me; for I wait on thee."

Psalm 146:5 (KJV) "Happy is he that hath the God of Jacob for his help, whose hope is in the Lord his God."

God's Promises of Provision

Matthew 6:33 (KJV) "But seek ye first the kingdom of God, and his righteousness; and all these things shall be added unto you."

2 Corinthians 9:8 (KJV) "And God is able to make all grace abound toward you; that ye, always having all sufficiency in all things, may abound to every good work."

Psalms - my summary of scripture.

1. Righteous of ungodly – life (life) – destroyed

2. Heathen thine inheritance – uttermost parts of earth – thy possession
Break them rod of iron / dash in pieces like a potter's vessel
Serve with fear – rejoice with trembling

3. Psalm of David – cried to the Lord arise O lord save me, Salvation belongeth to the Lord

4. Evening prayer for deliverance – trust in the Lord – no love for variety
I will lay me down in peace and sleep / the Lord maketh me safe

5. Morning prayer for guidance – the foolish shall not stand in thy sight – thou hatest all workers of iniquity – abhor the bloody and deceitful man – destroy them – your mercy – will worship in the temple

6. Prayer for God's mercy – don't rebuke or chastise in anger
Deliver my soul – punish my enemies – Lord will receive my prayer

7. Wickedness justly rewarded – Lord I put my trust in Thee
Forgive me – judge me by my good and not my bad
Righteous God, my summary of scripture continued.

8. God's glory and man's dominion – over work of Thy hands – O Lord how excellent is Thy Name in all the earth – who has set Thy Glory above heavens
Thou still the enemy and still the avenger – what is man – lower than the angels crowned with glory I honor – Lord how excellent it Thy Name in all the earth

9. Praise for victory over enemies / thou hast maintained my right and my cause – but the Lord will endure forever" He hath prepared His throne for judgement – in righteousness and for righteousness
Refuge for the oppressed, and refuse in times of trouble – my summary of scripture continued.
The wicked and the nations that forget God will be turned into Hell!
Nations are but men!

10. Petition for God's judgment – why stand far off – why hide in times of trouble / wicked persecute poor – will not seek after God – pride – conceit – cursing – fraud – mischief – vanity of the poor are His victims wicked and evil

11. God tests the children of men / Lord lovest righteousness His countenance doth behold the upright. If the foundations be destroyed what can the righteous do? Wicked and violence the Lord hates

12. The pure words of the Lord / the Lord will cut off all flattering lips and the tongue that speaketh proud things. For the oppression of the poor and the sighing of the needy, now will I rise said the Lord. The words of the Lord are pure

13. The prayer for God's answer – now – wilt thou forget me Tighten my eyes lest I sleep the sleep of death
I have trusted in Thy mercy my heart shall rejoice in Thy adoration

I will sing to the Lord because He hath dealt bountifully with me

14. The characteristics of the Godless – fools say there is no God
    Have the workers of inequity have no knowledge – and call not on the Lord
    The Lord looked down from Heaven upon the children of men to see if there were any who did understand and seek God

15. The characteristics of the Godly / wo shall dwell in Thy Holy hill worketh righteousness and speaketh truth in his heart
    Not biteth with his tongue or doeth evil to his neighbor
    He knows and fears the Lord - my summary of scripture continued.

16. Eternal life for one who trusts / I will bless the Lord who hath given me counsel / I have set the Lord before me / He is at my right hand.
    Why can't we all understand God wants us to follow His words? The reward is beyond human comprehension unless we ask Him for wisdom and understanding and commitment.

Purpose in Life

What is your purpose in life? Many of us don't know. Rest assured. God has a purpose for you to be here!! You may never know, but God knows. It may be dynamic, or inconsequential, but it's real.

The Holy Spirit can move you literally!! You are here for a reason. Some of us will not allow that purpose to happen because we turn away from God. However sometimes we fulfill a purpose for God, even though we are out of favor in God's eyes.

The main purpose for all of us is to prepare for the Kingdom of God, because He wants all His children to join Him in Heaven, but we must adhere to the rules of our Father.

Jude 1:1-25 (KJV) "1 Jude, the servant of Jesus Christ, and brother of James, to them that are sanctified by God the Father, and preserved in Jesus Christ, and called: 2 Mercy unto you, and peace, and love, be multiplied. 3 Beloved, when I gave all diligence to write unto you of the common salvation, it was needful for me to write unto you, and exhort you that ye should earnestly contend for the faith which was once delivered unto the saints. 4 For there are certain men crept in unawares, who were before of old ordained to this condemnation, ungodly men, turning the grace of our God into lasciviousness, and denying the only Lord God, and our Lord Jesus Christ. 5 I will therefore put you in remembrance, though ye once knew this, how that the Lord, having saved the people out of the land of Egypt, afterward destroyed them that believed not. 6 And the angels which kept not their first estate, but left their own habitation, he hath reserved in everlasting chains under darkness unto the judgment of the great day. 7 Even as Sodom and Gomorrah, and the cities about them in like manner, giving themselves over to fornication, and going after strange flesh, are set forth for an example, suffering the vengeance of eternal fire. 8 Likewise also these filthy dreamers defile the flesh, despise dominion, and speak evil of dignities. 9 Yet Michael the archangel, when contending with the devil he disputed about the body of Moses, durst not bring against him a railing accusation, but said, The Lord rebuke thee."

hapter 19

LET US PRAY THAT GOD DOES NOT REBUKE US. LET US PRAY FOR
wisdom to know what God expects from us.

Let us pray that Satan's temptations are not going to keep us
from the love God offers.

Let us pray that we don't weaken our ability to understand
God's wishes for us and know that His presence is always there.
We should know that, like Jonah, we can't hide from God. He's
always watching us, every awakened hour, and even when we're
asleep. Angels and the Holy Spirit are always there for us.

The reward for God's followers is so beautiful and peaceful
with no stress or pain or worries. What a nice goal to set for
ourselves. We may slip from time to time, but we can always get
"back in the game." Life is so pleasant when we give our problems
or needs over to God. Work like it's up to you but smile when He
does it for you.

God watches us daily and tries to help when we ask for it. When
there is unrest in our lives or in the world like the coronavirus, or
racial conflict, criminal behavior that comes from breaking the
law and an unfortunate injury or death occurs and injustice to

the perpetrator is glorified and the law overreacts unnecessarily, and anger causes others to suffer because protests and break-ins and destruction of property occurs, that affects innocent men and women. That's stupidity and Satan working.

We fought each other in the civil was to free the slaves. It wasn't color against color. It was white neighbors verses white neighbors. Black neighbors also fought for themselves. We are not a racist nation. We are a nation under God. Judeo-Christian principles formed our country. Why are we divided in the best country in the world? There is no better country anywhere with the opportunities we all have here.

There are injustices and prejudices, and probably always will be. Let's punish those people! But we're not enemies.

God tells us in Matthew 6:14-15, if you don't forgive, you can't be forgiven! That is my summary.

What you do to the least of my brothers, that is what I will do to you!!

Command demons, devils, and evil spirits to leave your presence, in the name of our Father, His Son Jesus, and God's Holy Spirit. Amen.

Temptations are all around us! God's love is all around us. God's love is everlasting. Temptation activity is a limited time. Then it's gone until the next sin.

You don't have to search for God. He's always right there.

Today it's so easy to ignore your Lord. So many things to do. So fortunate to use your excuses to forget to pay homage to your Maker. You do so much for others in your life, and they turn around and reject or ignore you. You can't understand how someone you've done so much for is not grateful or even say thanks??? What about God? You better hope you don't make God angry! The anger of the Lord is laid out very clearly in Nahum, chapter 1. The Lord notes: the guilty will be punished ... His power will cause you to tremble. Anyone who goes against God will be punished or destroyed.

God's power will be used to destroy what causes His anger. In 1 Corinthians 1, the spirit of love is in you! God has a plan for you! Are you ignoring it and following Satan without even knowing it? 1 Corinthians chapter 4. Ignore God's gifts. Verse 10, mistreating others? Chapter 6, you cannot judge others or call them names, like racists. Chapter 7, do not become slaves to anyone or to the government.

God wants you to follow Him and not Satan. Satan offers pleasure and material wealth and power. All are based on satisfaction of temporary desires and not long-lasting and can become boring or unsatisfying. It's not worth the loss of paradise for eternity. God's promises are so rewarding, and living by His rules is so satisfying, and He's there to see you through your life.

I feel sorry for you if you can't see this! I feel sorry for God if you don't also! Because His intentions are to fill His Heavens. The Lord never stops loving His children, even when they succumb to Satan.

How great and awesome that is!

The apostle Paul, as he completes a summary of the ultimate purposes of God, breaks into a hymn of praise (Romans 11:33-36). His words lift our gaze to our sovereign God whose ways are beyond our limited ability to understand or trace (verse 33). Yet the one who holds all things together in the heavens and on earth is intimately and lovingly involved with every detail of our lives (Matthew 6:25-34, and Colossians 1:16).

Even when things seem confusing, God's divine plans are unfolding for our good, and for God's honor and glory.

As human beings, we were created for community too (see Genesis 2:18, KJV). And in Ecclesiastes 4:10 (KJV), Solomon describes how vulnerable we are when we're alone: "Pity anyone who falls and has no one to help them up." There's strength in numbers, in summary he added, for "Though one may be overpowered, two can defend themselves. A cord of three strands in not quickly broken" (verse 12).

This is just as true for us spiritually as it is physically. God never intended for us to "fly" alone, vulnerably isolated. We need relationships with each other for encouragement, refreshment, and growth (see also 1 Corinthians 12:21).

God provides our needs.

hapter 20

Patriot - Man of God - should call you comrade because that's what communists call each other. That's where we are on our way. Battle of God against Satan. Communists don't believe in God.

You think you're victims now? Wait until the government controls you. You'll wish you hadn't been a part of riots, hating police, protecting and demonstrating for criminals. You're selling yourselves out! You're being used. You're being manipulated to divide our country. Look at yourselves, you're puppets. Black lives matter is giving lots of money to white democrats. You're out in the streets because they tell you to. They pay you to bring destruction and bring our country down. Yes, you are being led by those who want the government to own you. You're selling yourself into slavery. You're following the design to make us hate each other and cause social unrest and destroy our constitution all because you believe the lies they tell you.

The U.S. is not a racist country!! You're better off in America than any other country in the world!!! Why do you think people are desperate to come here? Figure it out. All the police actions may have been done by rogue cops, but don't blame all cops. Most of them are caring persons with families who are daily enforcing the law criminals are the ones to fear - not the police.

If government controls your life, even the egotistical celebrities will be begging to get our constitution back. Everyone gets a place to live an allowance for food and other items like clothes, transportation, and entertainment. Celebrities can't negotiate big money deals. Government control! Entertainers same, government controlled. Businesses run by government no big riches. Government control.

You think this uprising is about race. Don't be stupid. You are promoting the Satan-led campaign to get America away from one country under God!

I feel sorry for God that so many people try to support Satan in a country founded on Judeo-Christian principles now has those who will yield to the manipulation by Satan to undermine us and create socialism, which becomes communism, and then turns away from God. Will we finally ask God to help us?? Look at Cuba and Venezuela; take Hitler and Marx; countries targeted. They all succumbed to the lies and promises that will let themselves be taken over by the government; one which is certainly not for the people - of the people - or by the people! Only God can save us.

The Lord says, I have created the earth and the people. My expectations were worse than I expected. My summary in 1 Corinthians 13:13 (KJV), God reminds us that three things He gave us are faith, hope and love. The greatest of the three is love. God's love is everlasting! His hope was that ours would be also.

Why do some of us have so much difficulty in preserving our willingness to keep our love from being influenced by our environment and association with others? We sometimes almost look for ways to stifle love. Finding the least little thing, important or not, to get angry or rejectful of someone we love. It's almost like we want to interfere with the gift to love that God gave us to enjoy our lives! I think sometimes we want to punish ourselves by doing away with our greatest blessings. We perhaps think that there is more love and happiness somewhere or with someone else. If God isn't in the equation, there can never be total satisfaction!!!

Sometimes I think God feels like he's herding a bunch of cats, the way we bounce back and forth in our allegiance to Him. And how He has to remind us over and over that He is in charge. He is the all-powerful ruler over all things. He's always awake and always knows what we do. And how constant He is in watching us and knowing our thoughts and actions.

You should know that God plans who is in our lives. He knows our attitudes and our nature. He leads us to those we interact with, good or bad, and He sees how we react to evil and how we react to Him.

Good against evil.

God against Satan.

This is how He judges us and how He decides to give us another change or turn away from us. Oh, do I feel sorry for those God gives up on! Interestingly, He still gives us another chance … but we have to initiate the step back to God's blessings.

Pain can be for cleansing, or pain can be for punishment!

Chapter 21

Finality

NOW SINCE BEFORE HEAVENS AND EARTH WERE CREATED, WHICH was after Lucifer and his followers tried to undermine God's laws, we come to the beginning of the end of the human race as we know it. Especially the ones that yield and have yielded to Satan's efforts to turn God's subjects away from God's love and willingness to bring paradise to the masses. The Israelites born as God's people, and the United States founded in God's Judeo-Christian principles are being attacked by the powers of Satan.

The weakness of human lust and expectations of personal gratification. The willingness to be led to the slaughter by promises of easy living and self-serving pleasures promised by politicians supported by Satan.

God intended to prepare us for the Kingdom of Heaven. Living our lives providing for ourselves and our families by our own abilities and capabilities of the gifts and positions in life on our learning and work ethic, or birthright. He didn't intend to us all living the same kind of life, but according to circumstance and creativity. God's creativity made earth and mankind. God gives us our creativity to find our life.

Satan is now creating a society where many people want what someone else has created. They want something for nothing. Take someone's hard work and creativity and give it to the people who don't want to put out the effort to create their own lifestyle, but expect the government to support them or steal it from the successful. Get smart!! The government and the politicians can't offer or give you anything they don't take from someone else!!!

Those politicians promising you handouts are not giving you anything from their wealth. They keep what they have! They're selfish. Ask them to personally give to some of their assets and earnings and see what they say. They say no, the government will give it to you ... that's the people!! Your neighbors, their neighbors, the people who work hard and pay their taxes. Not the politicians' money ... other people's money. How many of them say: "You can get these entitlements and I'm giving half my wealth to make it happen." That is not what will happen!

No, Joe the butcher who opened his own business with doing without luxuries and saving enough to start his business while his friends were spending theirs on good times, nice cars, and living life to the fullest ... and now Joe has wealth and the high livers now want Joe to pay more so they can get some "freebies."

Socialism is coming. Just as soon as the lying politicians get elected. In a matter of time, the people will vote themselves into slavery to the government. Those who make the promises won't suffer. They'll enjoy controlling "you."

God won't feel sorry for "you."

God sent Jesus to cure our sins. Satan sends his followers to destroy this nation. You are led by evil to disrupt the greatest nation that has ever existed.

And: we're doing it to ourselves!!!

God have mercy.

God's wisdom and weaponry factuates the power and control over all things makes my feeling sorry for Him a moot point. But it doesn't keep me from feeling bad for Him. It's just so sad that all His children can't understand how much He wants to fill His Heavens that He created for us, all of us! The love and forgiving goes beyond any comprehension. It's mind-boggling and almost beyond believable. The most sinful and despiteful people that exist can be forgiven and repent. This is a difficult position of understanding to realize how some terrible people can become disciples of God. They can help convert more people who have lost their way.

Don't ever look at a convert and say, "I know him or her and they have done some terrible sins and now they want to present themselves as God's disciple?" Well, yes, they can. Some of the worst sinners can become great servants of the Lord. Look at Paul, John Newton, Matthew, almost all of us have sins we wish we didn't have since we have found the love of Jesus and our Lord. Maybe that makes them stronger in their mission for God. If you've been bad in your life, you know how to approach those who are bad now because you've been there, my summary as in Ephesians and Corinthians 1 verse 2.

God's wisdom is hidden until God releases it! To those who love Him. Through visions, some of it comes to those He wants to share!!!

I am one of the fortunate ones who God communicates with through dreams and visions. He has used me to build the Shrine of the Holy Spirit in Branson, Missouri. He has used my hands to write messages and two books about Him. He now has given me the incentive to help bring this country back to One Nation Under Him. Organizations and gangs that do Satan's work (politicians included), Black Lives Matter is using and being used for Satan's attempt to destroy our country. Antifa is their destructive arm.

Good against evil. God versus Satan.

What side are you on??

Family B

I was born into this world as the son of Roy and Ellen Bicknell (Orval Leroy and Martha Elena Grazier Bicknell).

My life began a mile outside of Picher, Oklahoma, a town born out of the discovery of lead and zinc in northeastern Oklahoma.

Our family was poor, and we were seven children, of which I was next to last. There was 19 years between the oldest and the youngest of us. There was no religion in our house. Dad said he didn't believe in God, but we found him reading the bible in his later years. Mom never prayed or mentioned God or Christ, but when I prayed and found the strength to mention baptism to her, the Holy Spirit came upon me and I was moved and the Spirit moved my mom and she agreed to join the church and be baptized; and I hardly had to do anything. The baptism happened by the help of a priest. I baptized my dad myself later. Other family members came to be saved and spiritual after that. I was an adult with a family when those things happened.

The belief and desire to know God came early for me. I had a firm feeling that God was real, and I wanted to know Him.

Our home had no discussion of faith and none of us acted like Christians. At age 15 after going to church with other friends and families, I decided I wanted to be baptized and join a church. I got baptized on a Sunday evening and went home excited and full of pride. After telling my parents, I was deflated because they rebutted the effort and the unimportance of church.

My life after 15 wasn't that committed to God totally, and I sinned repeatedly, but I never lost my firm belief in God, Jesus, and the Holy Spirit. Girls, parties, and some profanity was easy for me, but I wasn't extreme in any of those. My love of God was always present but not confirmed.

At age 23 I got married and joined the Catholic Church; had babies and was active in the church. A divorce 19 years later left me rejected from the sacraments if I remarried. So when 20 years later when I remarried, Rita and I became members of another denomination.

I have been praying for 37 years now, usually 20 or 30 minutes a day.

I still pray daily and all these years I prayed for my children and grandchildren, also my friends and people who I know to have problems or medical needs. My prayers are seldom for myself except to give thanks for blessings given to those I care about.

You can't out give God! I found that early on when I borrowed money to give to the church because I hadn't been able to give as much as I thought I should. God saw that I Got it back tenfold just as the Holy Spirit worked to save my mom. He has been with me many times and I live with the Holy Spirit every day. His hands are on me!

Through the years I've sinned, but never without regret!

Today and for many years now, I don't sin intentionally, and I can't think of any unintentionally, but probable some way in just thought. My comfort level in serving God is extremely high and helping others has always been a way of life with me.

Epilogue

I WAS A SERVANT WHO WROTE THIS BOOK FOR GOD. HE GAVE ME the inspiration and led my writing His message.

Honor and appreciation for being able to do this is filling me with gratitude and pride to be given this opportunity. My faith can bring me to tears when I think about what my Heavenly Father has done for me and my family!

We are so blessed and so undeserving that the Holy Spirit lifts me to tears.

My ministry is God's worker. All profits from "I Feel Sorry for God" and "The Personal Side of God" go to God's work and charities. None given to anything other than for helping those in need or God's purposes. It goes into an account for God's intentions.

Our challenge is to reach the non-believers.

Heaven will be like the Garden of Eden. My wife, Rita, is there now and I've seen her in vision when I was wide awake! Music and beauty with no pain, no worries. We will all love each other and we'll see God, Jesus and live in the presence of them and enjoy the Holy Spirit as many of us do here on Earth.

Postlude

BEING A PATRIOT AND BEING A CHRISTIAN IS ALMOST THE SAME. We're in a war! Good against evil. God against Satan. Satan uses us by causing differences between us. Black against white. Political parties and false statement to lie and deceive.

Satan wants to bring down America and cause the U.S. to fail. Take away our freedom. Our way of life, our opportunities in the greatest nation that ever existed and change it to communism, which doesn't believe in God.

Many people are being used by Satan to support those people who want to destroy us!

Evil billionaires and celebrities find themselves serving Satan and their egotistical ideas of socialism and leaving God out of their plans. In Isaiah 29 and 30, a summary of my views after reading the scripture, God says they will be punished and crushed.

Our society is not perfect, but we're founded under God and He wants us to be worthy of His love.

My ancestors were the only people in this country until the settlers arrived. Now we're all Americans.

Let's follow my Matthew 6:14-15 summary ... and forgive or not be forgiven.

In Appreciation

I WANT TO THANK ALL THOSE WHO CONTRIBUTED TO THIS BOOK. First God's encouragement and my desire to help everyone to understand what God goes through from His creation! His never-ending love and desire for us to share His Kingdom. The forgiveness of our sins and inequities. The chance after chance for repentance and follow His Laws and worship. The Chosen People to accept Jesus as The Son of God. Even to the end of the 1000 years of the Rule of Jesus on the New Earth God will accept us as His Followers. How His assignment of Responsibility to His Son as we on earth now pass responsibility to our sons and daughters. God's unbelievable forgiveness after being offended and ignored for so long! Thanks to Shelly Burgan for her editing, typing, and organizing structure of this work. God put the words and meanings in our heads. This is God's telling us of His Deep Love for His Creation. Thanks for reading, Gene B.

Printed in the United States
by Baker & Taylor Publisher Services